Dept of Economics. '25.

THEORIES OF THE TRADE CYCLE

MACMILLAN AND CO., Limited
LONDON · BOMBAY · CALCUTTA · MADRAS
MELBOURNE

THE MACMILLAN COMPANY
NEW YORK · BOSTON · CHICAGO
DALLAS · ATLANTA · SAN FRANCISCO

THE MACMILLAN COMPANY
OF CANADA, LIMITED
TORONTO

THEORIES

OF

THE TRADE CYCLE

BY

ALEC L. MACFIE, M.A., LL.B.

LECTURER IN POLITICAL ECONOMY
UNIVERSITY OF GLASGOW

MACMILLAN AND CO., LIMITED
ST. MARTIN'S STREET, LONDON
1934

COPYRIGHT

PRINTED IN GREAT BRITAIN
BY R. & R. CLARK, LIMITED, EDINBURGH

PREFACE

THE transition from static to dynamic economic theory, or from the long to the short period, is notoriously difficult. The difficulties concentrate in the explanation of the trade cycle. In lieu of a better, this book is an endeavour to smooth the passage, especially for young students. Those who have not been discouraged by one year in the subject may find it a useful introduction to a second. I therefore assume a knowledge of the static theory, including therein a general comprehension of the working monetary system. To simplify the argument, I have not worked out in detail the qualifications introduced by the fact that trade also moves over national frontiers. It is important that the general principles should first be grasped. So to these I have confined my efforts.

In trade-cycle theory we are still in the age of exploration. Modern pioneers, especially those I try to interpret, have done heroic work in blazing the trails. But pioneers should not also be expected to lay smooth pathways for their followers. I have attempted to lay such a pathway.

To make it manageable the field has been limited to works published in Britain. The texts I deal with are undoubtedly difficult; and the prevalence of mathematical exposition must render them especi-

v

ally arduous to many young economists. I have therefore avoided such formulae. It has been argued that complaints about the mathematical exposition of economics are as unreasonable as criticisms of a foreign literature by one ignorant of the language. And certainly those on the frontiers should not be limited in any way. But if the analogy is pressed too far, it should be maintained that translations of foreign languages also have their uses.

I am of course entirely responsible for the interpretations I offer. Each may be an inacceptable gloss on its author. But the remedy is to read the texts. If this book encourages such references its purpose will be accomplished.

In view of the book's arrangement and character, the provision of an analytical table of contents renders the addition of an index unnecessary.

There remains the pleasant opportunity of thanking those who have given me generous help. Professor W. R. Scott's constant encouragement has been a happy inspiration to endeavour. To Mr. D. T. Jack, M.A., Lecturer in Economics, St. Andrews University, my debt is immense. His detailed and always constructive criticism afforded me a continuing incentive to persevere. He also shared the correction of the proofs with Mr. James Cunnison, M.A., and Mr. J. W. Nisbet, M.A., LL.B., both Lecturers in the Department of Political Economy, Glasgow University. That is indeed a token of friendly altruism.   A. L. M.

THE UNIVERSITY
   GLASGOW

CONTENTS

CHAPTER I

THE FACTS AND THE PROBLEM

CHAPTER II

"REAL" CAUSES OF RHYTHM

CHAPTER III

MONETARY

CHAPTER IV

RATES OF INTEREST

vii

CHAPTER V

CHAPTER VI

CHAPTER VII

CHAPTER VIII

CHAPTER IX

PSYCHOLOGICAL

CHAPTER X

SYNTHESIS

APPENDICES

THE FACTS AND THE PROBLEM

1. SINCE modern capitalistic methods were introduced into industry, economic activity has developed, certainly at an irregular rate, but also at a rate the irregularity of which seems yet to have obeyed some law. In a word production appears to have grown rhythmically in alternate curves above and below an upward trend.[1] By "capitalistic" is meant that system under which independent enterprisers have directed the flow of labour and savings made dominantly by others into varying types of investment. This appearance of rhythm can be illustrated by a host of different statistical sequences, some of which will be briefly considered.

In this country the unemployment records are more satisfactory than other figures, chiefly because we have a fair sample of such figures up to 1922 in the trade-union returns, and a very full sample after 1922 in the official statistics. They also illustrate directly what is steadily becoming the most important social problem arising from industrial fluctuations. Of course when we consider unemployment figures within a fairly short period we

[1] Where rhythm is used in future some *regularity* in the fluctuations is implied.

have to remember that in such a period the ultimate harmonies of long-period tendencies have no room to assert themselves. For instance, the effects on unemployment of a rapid increase in the introduction of labour-saving machinery may be much more serious in one fairly short period than in another, say, thirty years earlier or later. This accounts to some extent for the heavier average percentage of unemployed in post-war years as compared with the period 1860 to 1914. Such uniquely industrialised countries as the United States, Germany and Britain are bound to feel the effects of this longer-period invention trend especially severely. But this trend is outside the short-period cycle problem.

The figures, which will be found in Appendix 1, have not been taken before 1860; first, because our aim is to introduce theories, not to exhaust the facts, so that the most suitable facts best suit our purpose; and secondly because, as Sir William Beveridge has pointed out, the trends before 1860 are not so typical of the movement we wish to understand as they are after that date. Starting then at 1860 we can summarise the figures in the Table opposite.

Between any of the successive years in alternate tables the movement of unemployment was regular in the sense that there was an unbroken rise from the low year 1860, for instance, to the high year 1862, followed by an unbroken fall from the high year 1862 to the low year 1865; and so on. The fact that the figures are yearly averages should prevent us from putting too exact an interpretation on them. But yearly averages at least eliminate seasonal fluctuations.

Years of Lowest Unemployment	Period between (years)	Years of Highest Unemployment	Period between (years)
1860		1862	
1865	5	1868	6
1872	7	1879	11
1882	10	1886	7
1889	7	1893	7
1899	10	1904	11
1906	7	1909	5
1913	7		

There have been so many disturbing influences since the war that tabulation of post-war figures on these lines would be misleading. The figures show steady improvement after the rapid (and untypical) post-war boom and slump. But this improvement up to 1929 was interrupted by the disturbance of the £'s value due to the return to gold in 1925, and by the strike of 1926. The events since 1929 we need not record. Unfortunately they show that the pre-war instability has reasserted itself.

Further, as to unemployment, its varying intensities in different industries should be mentioned. For instance, in pre-war times the percentage unemployed of the group, engineering, shipbuilding and metals, showed an interesting tendency to approximate closely to the general percentage un-

employed so far as years of low unemployment
were concerned; but in the high years of unemployment this capitalistic group's figures ruled heavily
and steadily above the general index. The conditions
are different in the consumption or finishing industries.[1] But this fact will be directly illustrated later
by post-war figures of employment. In all industries,
however, the swing over from rising to falling unemployment takes place at approximately the same
time, if long-period trends are allowed for.

As to variations in the level of prices, the Board
of Trade Index from 1870 to 1913 gives the following results if treated as before:

Years of Highest Prices	Years of Lowest Prices
1873	1879
1880	1887
1891	1896
1900	1902
1907	1908
1913	

From these figures the secular trend of prices is not
eliminated and therefore care should be taken before conclusions are drawn from comparisons with
similar unemployment figures. The long-period
trend in prices, for instance, has been mainly determined from the monetary side by the supply of
gold. And this trend has no exact connection with
the long-period trend in the introduction of inventions. Again, temporary disturbances in price-levels

[1] The figures will be found in Pigou, *Industrial Fluctuations*
Appendix, Table I. p. 353.

do not coincide with similar disturbances in employment.[1]

As to international price-levels, Sir Walter Layton has compared the British wholesale index with
similar indices for Germany and the United States.[2]
The resultant graph shows that this rhythmical
movement in activity overflows national bound-
aries (so far as wholesale prices truly interpret it),
and affects similarly at least those countries which
are linked by trade and have reached a similar
stage in industrial development. Of course one
would expect a high correlation of wholesale prices
as between countries all maintaining the gold
standard. For the goods which enter these indices
constitute in the main a world market. They have
approximately the same gold price in any country,
so that their price-levels in terms of currencies
which are bound to gold must fluctuate together.
But these correlations do indicate that fluctuations
affect similarly countries with developed trade
relations. They are an index of the world trade
cycle. Professor Mitchell's investigations led him
to conclude on this topic that "the international
influences are gaining in relative importance".[3]
Events since 1929 may seem to qualify his conclusion. But this should not be assumed too rapidly.

---

[1] The index of prices will be found in Appendix 2. Students who
wish to consult a more refined examination of the trend of prices
are referred to Pigou, *Industrial Fluctuations*, p. 118 and the
relevant chart.

[2] Appendix 2.

[3] *Business Cycles* (1927), p. 450.

It is at least apparent that the depth of the slump coincides to a definite extent with the destruction of that level of international trade which is now necessary for economic health.

2. We have not so far illustrated the post-war fluctuations. This can now be done in a more varied way than was possible in pre-war days; for various indices of production have been made available by the League of Nations Economic Intelligence Service. The more important figures—in summarised form—will serve our purpose.

TABLE I [1]

INDEX OF INDUSTRIAL PRODUCTION FOR WORLD, EXCLUDING
U.S.S.R.

(Base: 1925–1929 = 100)

1925	1926	1927	1928	1929	1930	1931	1932
93	94	100	103	110	96	84	69

TABLE II

INDEX-NUMBERS OF INDUSTRIAL RAW MATERIAL PRODUCTION,
WEIGHTED BY 1930 VALUES

(Base: 1925–1929 = 100)

	1925	1929	1930	1931	1932
Europe, excluding U.S.S.R.	90	117	102	90	80
North America . . .	94	108	94	82	61
Africa	95	112	109	95	90

[1] Particulars as to these indices will be found in *World Production and Prices*, 1925–32.

TABLE III

WORLD PRODUCTION OF RAW MATERIALS, EXCLUDING U.S.S.R.

(Base: 1925–1929 = 100)

	1925	1929	1930	1931	1932
Raw materials for producers' goods	91	112	98	81	66
Raw materials for consumers' goods . .	98	102	102	103	100

Several interesting comments arise. First, there is the natural assumption that the indices represent a cyclical movement of the same nature as those which took place before the war. Certainly the onus of proof is on those who contest this conclusion. Secondly, the fact that the amplitude for North America is the greatest, that for Africa the least, supports the view that the extent of the swings depends on the stage of development reached. (It does not therefore follow that the African economy is the best!) Thirdly, Table III. illustrates the fact that the swings are much more severe in the capital industries than in the consumption industries. Both expansion and contraction are much more extreme in the former. It must not, however, be concluded that the consumption industries were prosperous in the slump. This is the reverse of the truth. The consumption industries are mainly agricultural in origin. Agricultural gold prices have slumped more heavily in world markets than those of most other types of goods. In the first quarter of 1933 cereals and other foodstuffs were 50 to 70 per cent. below the 1929 level; animal foodstuffs were 40 to 60 per cent. lower; whereas coal had fallen by only 35 per cent.[1] Of course the particular reason for this discrepancy is the inelasticity of agricultural supply, in face of a slump in demand, in the fairly short period. But this only intensifies agricultural depression. The figures support the assumption that a turning point in agricultural activity has coincided with the general turning point. Finally, it should be noted that the long-period trend is not eliminated from these figures. The productive capacity of the system expands in the long period, though actual production fluctuates (perhaps rhythmically) above and below the trend of production. The fact that the output of consumable goods remains fairly steady in depressions and grows in prosperity must not blind us to the fact that the cycle imposes irreparable social losses. For while improvement in methods realises greater production per unit of effort applied, the reverse side of the shield is shown by the unemployment figures. The different indices should therefore be visualised as complementary to the complete picture.

Finally, as to illustrative statistics, Sir William Beveridge's "synthetic chart"[2] should be pondered. Its great merit is that it shows graphically, in fact dramatically, the ubiquity of this social "pulse's"

---

[1] The fall in *internal* agricultural prices was not nearly so heavy, because of the protective measures taken. But these were adopted mainly to meet the specially depressing conditions there. The figures are taken from the *World Economic Survey*, 1932–33, p. 52.

[2] Beveridge, *Unemployment*, facing p. 341.

beat, in its many forms. Bank rate, foreign trade, wholesale prices, Budget results, employment, the marriage rate, indoor pauperism, consumption of beer, flotation of companies, all seem to swing to the same tune. Is there a tune? Is there an inherent rhythm? Certainly the broad sympathy of movement demands an enquiry as to the possibility of a logical explanation.

The chart's reference to social factors also underlines some of the social evils that the trail of the cycle leaves. The purely material losses involved as against a steady harmonious expansion are evident enough. But, socially, fluctuations in income are double-barrelled for evil. For, first, there is the loss caused by the fact that a steadily expanding income must by the law of diminishing utility yield more utility than an income which fluctuates about that steady trend.[1] And, secondly, there is the loss arising from the fact of variation in income itself. The art of consumption is a plant of slow growth. It depends on wise spending, which in turn springs from qualities of mind, emotion and body. If income expands suddenly wisdom cannot follow it, and there is waste. So both the up-swings and the down-swings generate their own type of waste in welfare. If we could control these fluctuations we should avoid much vicious vulgarity, as well as much poverty.

[1] For it follows from the law of diminishing utility that the loss in utility through a regularly fluctuating income falling below the trend exceeds the gain in utility through the fluctuating income rising above the trend.

3. The facts can next be examined more analytically by considering certain characteristics of industrial fluctuations. From this point of view Professor Wesley C. Mitchell's *Business Cycles* offers a rich store, which will be largely drawn on.

First comes the question of the period between successive crests (or troughs) of the cycles, or their duration. The most useful summary for our purposes given by Professor Mitchell is reproduced below.

FREQUENCY DISTRIBUTION OF BUSINESS CYCLES ACCORDING TO DURATION IN YEARS [1]

Duration in Years	England, 1793–1920	Germany, 1848–1925	United States, 1796–1923
1 year. . .	..	..	1
2 years . .	2	1	4
3 ,, . .	1	4	10
4 ,, . .	5	4	5
5 ,, . .	2	1	6
6 ,, . .	4	1	4
7 ,, . .	2	..	1
8 ,, . .	3	1	..
9 ,, . .	1	2	1
10 ,, . .	2	1	..
Total number .	22	15	32
Average duration in years . .	5·8	5·1	4·0

As to the variations in the lengths of cycles round the average duration, it will be sufficient, for purposes of illustration, to quote Professor Mitchell's conclusions on the United States figures for the period 1878–1923. "They are far from uniform in duration, but their durations are distributed about

[1] *Op. cit.* p. 398.

a well-marked central tendency in a tolerably regular fashion."[1]

It should further be noted that within any one cycle the rise to the crest and the fall to the trough do not proceed at an even pace. After the turning point the recession is generally rapid, just as is the revival once the upward move definitely begins. "Put together," says Professor Mitchell,[2] "the phases of recession and revival account for only one-quarter of the duration of business cycles on the average. Of the remaining three-quarters, the prosperous phase occupies a somewhat longer time than the phase of depression."[3]

Secondly, there is the extent to which industrial activity rises above or falls below its long-period trend. As to these amplitudes Professor Mitchell has examined indices for the United States cycles between 1879 and 1923. The "grand average"[4] of all the percentage rises above and declines below the trend values is 25·5 per cent. This includes departures as great as 45 to 50 per cent. from the trend. Professor Mitchell also notes that "on the whole our frequency distributions of the amplitudes of cyclical fluctuations are somewhat more regular than our distributions of their durations, and afford even less basis for supposing that there are two or more distinct species of business cycles".[5] Of course, averages should be treated with the utmost caution. For instance, this average flattens out much larger

<hr>

[1] *Op. cit.* p. 343.   [2] *Op. cit.* p. 420.   [3] But compare p. 14.
    [4] *Op. cit.* p. 353.   [5] *Op. cit.* p. 352.

swings in some trades than in others. Professor Mitchell illustrates this from the depression of 1921–22. "Manufacturing, railroading, mining and construction work were most disastrously affected by the depression. A second group, in which the shrinkage of employment was far less serious, but substantial, included finance, wholesale trade and transportation other than by railroad. These two groups of industries constitute the sphere of business par excellence. The remaining industries, among them agriculture and retailing, are characterised by small-scale organisation, or by the prominence of non-commercial aims, or by both features. These industries reduced the amount of employment offered but slightly."[1] Professor Pigou has also illustrated these variations between the activity of different industries from the British pre-war unemployment figures.[2] A more recent example is reproduced, on page 13, from the *Economist*.

The Heavy Trade index includes coal-mining, the metal trades, and shipbuilding. The rapid drop in 1926 is, of course, principally due to the General Strike; and the rise in 1927 should therefore be considerably discounted. The Distributive Trades index comprises clothing, transport and public utilities, food, drink and tobacco, and of course the distributive trades themselves. The index for all trades acts as a useful complement to the more depressing unemployment index. For it shows that as far as total employment goes the failure since 1924 has con-

[1] *Op. cit.* p. 87.   [2] *Industrial Fluctuations*, p. 16.

sisted in lack of progress, or inability to absorb a
growing population. But this once more ignores the

(Employment: 1924 = 100) [1]

Year	All Trades	Heavy Trades	Distributive Trades, etc.
1920	105	..	..
1921	90	..	..
1922	94	..	..
1923	$97\frac{1}{2}$	..	..
1924	100	100	100
1925	$100\frac{3}{4}$	$89\frac{1}{2}$	103
1926	$99\frac{3}{4}$	57	104
1927	105	87	$108\frac{1}{2}$
1928	105	82	$109\frac{1}{2}$
1929	107	$84\frac{1}{2}$	$112\frac{1}{2}$
1930	$102\frac{3}{4}$	$77\frac{1}{2}$	$112\frac{1}{2}$
1931	99	$65\frac{3}{4}$	$114\frac{1}{2}$
1932	$98\frac{1}{2}$	$59\frac{1}{2}$	116
1933	102	61	119

most intractable element in the problem, which,
however, the Heavy Trade index underlines: the
very heavy fall in employment in some trades, combined with the inadequacy of industrial mobility.

Thirdly, we must note an important contrast
which has been clarified by Dr. Thorp, of the
National Bureau of Economic Research. He has
established that, when the secular trend of prices
has been upward, the number of years of prosperity
has exceeded that of the years of depression. When
the secular price trend has been downwards, the
opposite has obtained. The facts are as follows:

[1] *Economist*, October 21, 1933, and July 28, 1934.

[TABLE

RELATIVE DURATION OF THE PROSPEROUS AND THE DEPRESSED PHASES OF
BUSINESS CYCLES IN PERIODS OF RISING AND DECLINING TRENDS OF
WHOLESALE PRICES [1]

ENGLAND	Years of Prosperity per year of Depression	UNITED STATES	Years of Prosperity per year of Depression
1790–1815: prices rising	1·0	1790–1815: prices rising	2·6
1815–1849: prices falling	0·9	1815–1849: prices falling	0·8
1849–1873: prices rising	3·3	1849–1865: prices rising	2·9
1873–1896: prices falling	0·4	1865–1896: prices falling	0·9
1896–1920: prices rising	2·7	1896–1920: prices rising	3·1

This table forms an interesting commentary on
the Marxian socialist view[2] that the ravages of
economic crises will tend to increase as the capitalistic system develops. The table in itself does not of
course confute the prophecy. But it suggests that
the tendency is not inevitable. For if a falling
secular price trend can be avoided, the years of
depression can be sensibly reduced. The less hide-
bound attitude to currency control which has
grown out of the gold shortage controversy, and
recent manipulations of currencies, indicate that a
falling long-period trend need not be regarded as a
law of nature. There seems no reason why we
should not learn to avoid it.

This summary of facts is of course in no sense
comprehensive. For such an analysis the student
should repair to Professor Mitchell's volume. Our
interest is primarily in theories. But a broad out-

[1] Mitchell, *op. cit.* p. 411.

[2] Cf. Hyndman, *Economics of Socialism*, Lecture V., or Lenin,
Imperialism, ch. i.

line in perspective, a representative sample of the facts, seems a necessary introduction to the examination of their explanations.

4. What are we to make of these facts?

There may, of course, be no problem.[1] But that is rather a conclusion to which to return if we can find no reason for believing that there are some common causes at work. For, as the facts stand, the obvious initial assumption is that some such causes exist. The lengths of the cycles, the distribution of their amplitudes, and also the fact that the turning periods of so many different industrial activities approximately coincide, impose on any impartial observer the obligation to examine the hypothesis of common causation.

We should, however, be clear on the definition of the hypothesis we are to examine. Professor Mitchell, for instance, insists that such regularity as appears does not justify defining it as "periodicity". For, as he says, "the time intervals between crises are far from regular".[2] Again, he tells us that "students of the business cycles . . . speak of cyclical fluctuations instead of periodic fluctuations, just because the first term does not imply strict regularity of recurrence".[3] Certainly if periodicity means strict regularity the term should be avoided. But this just puts the problem in another form.

[1] Cf. Irving Fisher in *Journal of the American Statistical Association*, June 1925.
[2] *Op. cit.* p. 378.   [3] *Op. cit.* p. 467.

What do we mean by cyclical? "A measure of regularity"[1] is certainly implied. So we must start, as Professor Mitchell says, with "the fundamental fact of rhythmical fluctuations in activity".[2] For the curves, while not absolutely regular, still strongly suggest rhythm.

Yet it is not clear that Professor Mitchell considers rhythm to be the essence of the actual fluctuations. The regularity that appears is not "strict regularity of timing" but rather "the recurrence of prosperity, recession, depression and revival, in that sequence".[3] His final statement is this. "There are enough series which show tolerably regular cyclical fluctuations, agreeing with one another, and with our business annals in tenor, to give us confidence in the *basic element* of our conception— the recurrence of the prosperity—recession—depression—revival sequence."[4] Of course the presence of some rhythm is here maintained. But in the reaction against the idea of absolute regularity it seems possible that a false antithesis may have been suggested. For "tolerable" regularity must be present, and may be more of the essence of cycles than the regular sequence of stages. In fact it is difficult to see why the latter regular sequence should be regarded as of their essence at all. For if you draw any curve of industrial activity, at random and totally irregular, it would be perfectly possible to divide it into these four stages following

[1] *Op. cit.* p. 468.   [2] *Op. cit.* p. 458.
[3] *Op. cit.* p. 454.   [4] *Op. cit.* p. 464, italics mine.

each other in invariable sequence. Yet no one could argue that such a curve illustrated the essence of the facts we wish to understand. It must therefore be this "tolerable" regularity which our theories endeavour to explain.

It is perhaps worth noting here the results of an investigation by Dr. Mills which Professor Mitchell quotes.[1] They show that cycles vary in duration according to the stage of industrial development reached by the community in question.

England	.	1793–1831	9	cycles.	Average	duration	4·22	years.
,,	.	1831–1920	13	,,	,,	,,	6·85	,,
France	.	1854–1876	6	,,	,,	,,	3·67	,,
,,	.	1876–1920	7	,,	,,	,,	6·32	,,
United States		1796–1822	5	,,	,,	,,	5·20	,,
,,	,,	1822–1860	11	,,	,,	,,	3·50	,,
,,	,,	1860–1888	5	,,	,,	,,	5·50	,,
,,	,,	1888–1923	11	,,	,,	,,	3·20	,,

These figures go far to establish the fact that, while a country is developing rapidly, cycles are more numerous than over a period when it has reached comparative stability.[2] But does not this support the view that the actual regularity of the *cyclical* movement is greater than an average for all cycles would indicate? For the various long-period stages of development are extraneous to the regularity of the cycles *within* them.

The point of view of four stages in invariable sequence is, however, valuable. For a problem would

[1] *Op. cit.* p. 415.

[2] Of course the average durations depend on the decisions as to the periods, which would almost certainly differ with different authorities. But this does not affect the broad truth of the analysis.

certainly arise for examination if we assumed that
one stage *invariably leads* to the next in that order:
that prosperity invariably leads to recession which
is invariably followed by depression, which in turn
breeds revival. The problem would be: what is the
cause or logic of this sequence? But this statement
is also inadequate to the facts. We have to ask
what is the cause of this invariable and fairly
regular sequence? There is both sequence and
rhythm; or at least if either is absent there is no
cyclical problem to theorise about. The facts suggest that there is some self-generative force running
through these fluctuations. Cyclical movements re-
semble the swings of a pendulum. Once it has been
set in movement, the swing to the right itself
generates the force which will cause the recession,
then the swing to the other extreme, and so on.
This is what is meant by rhythm; and rhythm includes the idea of an invariable sequence of stages.

So we justify our examination of trade-cycle
theories broadly as follows. As the facts stand, the
hypothesis they most clearly suggest is that there
is some rhythmic force operating in modern business communities to generate fairly regular cycles
of activity and depression. What that force may be
can be discovered only by theories which logically
explain the sequences. Just as the properties of
electricity have been worked out by starting from a
comprehensive hypothesis and developing it logically in constant relation to the facts, so here we can
advance only by examining different definitions of

this rhythmic force and comparing the extent to
which they explain the facts, and the logic with
which they do so. In sum, our theories simply try
to define the logical dynamics of the actual movements. On their success depends the conclusion as
to whether the hypothesis of rhythm is justified.

So to the theories we shall turn.

Duration of Cycle.

UK.	USA.
7.46	9.35
7.05	7.74
8.13	8.54
8.69	10.23
8.89	9.35
10.46	9.70
9.04	8.71
8.57	7.31
9.07	8.59
8.10	7.87
8.83	8.72
9.85	10.56
9.31	10.09
7.39	9.16
6.67	6.14

Av.	8.49	8.80
St. Dev.	1.02	1.15

CHAPTER II

"REAL" CAUSES OF RHYTHM

1. REAL causes are those which arise out of objective or actual factors in industry, as against subjective or psychologically directed influences. Monetary
causes are usually given separate consideration,
although of course they are also real. How far, then,
can actual conditions cause a pervasive rhythmic
rise and fall in the volume of total output?

There is a considerable list of such causes; but
variations in the weather and in the rate of inventions are of such outstanding importance that we
can confine ourselves to them.[1]

Agricultural output varies from year to year. It
has further been argued, first, that this variation
in volume is itself rhythmic, and secondly that this
rhythm is the main, or a dominant cause of the
rhythm in total output. W. S. Jevons set this ball
rolling in 1875 when he adopted the astronomical
deduction that there is a ten-year period in solar
heat caused by regular variations in sun-spots. The
recurring inadequacies in heat he connected with
ten-yearly famines in India, and also in tropical
regions generally, though the latter correlation he

[1] For a fuller discussion consult Pigou, *Industrial Fluctuations*,
ch. iv.

20

suggested rather than proved. The repercussion of this agricultural cycle on the volume of Eastern trade with the West set the flame or gave the cold douche to speculation at home.

Now it is highly probable that rhythm in agricultural output exists; but there are definite reasons for doubting whether this rhythm is caused by weather conditions. Firstly, there is the lack of unanimity as to the length of "weather cycles".[1] Shortly after Jevons adopted the ten-yearly cycle, the meteorologists rather unkindly lengthened their period to eleven years. In 1909, Jevons's son, Professor H. S. Jevons, tried to fit a cycle of three and a half years in agricultural output to a similar cycle in barometric pressure. In 1914, Professor H. L. Moore sought to establish a connection between an eight-year rainfall cycle and output for grain areas in the United States. Dr. Shaw suggests an eleven-year periodicity in the yield of wheat in eastern England. Sir William Beveridge's examination of evidence between 1545 and 1844 indicates that there are many cycles in the weather.[2]

It is possible, of course, that all these deductions as to the lengths of weather cycles may yet be reconciled. But when we compare them as they stand with the rhythmic facts of total output, and there is no doubt about the lengths of these periods, we must conclude that it cannot be proved that the

[1] Cf. Pigou, *op. cit.* p. 211; also J. H. Kirk, *Agriculture and the Trade Cycle*, p. 168.
[2] *Journal of the Royal Statistical Society*, May 1922.

weather cycle causes the total output cycle. The
case is as yet not proven. The figures we have
considered as to the effect of the stage of industrial
development on the lengths of trade cycles afford
an additional hurdle to "weather" explanations.
For the weather has not been shown to undergo
similar stages of development. The conclusion
therefore emerges that while weather cycles would
affect cycles in agricultural output, the further
argument that they control cycles in total output
cannot be admitted. It would, of course, be true that
where movements of total and agricultural output
tended in the same direction the momentum of
harvest volumes would intensify that of total output: and where total output was, for instance, showing signs of recovery from a slump a bumper harvest
would affect the *time* at which recovery would take
place. There is considerable backing, however, for
the belief that harvest variations are not sufficient
to check contrary variations in the volume of total
output.[1]

The facts support this interpretation. There are
clear reasons why the effects of agricultural variations should diminish relatively. The variations in
agricultural supplies that could be available to any
one country, or to the world as a whole, are themselves diminishing. The development of communication, of storage methods (including speculation),
of irrigation, and of disease-resisting crops all tend
this way. Further, primary products constitute a

---

[1] Pigou, *op. cit.* p. 40.

decreasing proportion of total output. Thus, Jevons was so far justified, as he based his theory on the period up to 1860, when primary products were relatively more important than they are to-day. It has in fact been argued that the more advanced nations have now reached the tertiary historical stage, when personal and distributive services are steadily growing in relative weight, as compared with the primary stage when agriculture preponderates, and the secondary phase when capitalistic manufacture takes precedence.[1]

One further remark should be added, to prevent misconception. The argument proferred is, of course, directed only against the claim that regular changes in atmospheric conditions can explain the trade cycle. It does not affect the contention that the conditions of production in agriculture may have an important influence on the course of the major cycles. But the latter view is not here developed because it is a specialist enquiry; and also because it employs, no doubt with unique weighting, arguments which apply in the examination of industrial activity generally.[2] These arguments will be examined in their larger setting. Thus, for instance, the fact that variations in agricultural output are affected by its seasonal nature, and that therefore planned increases in such output may take as long as two years to reach the consumer, has definite

[1] Cf. article by A. G. B. Fisher in *Economic Journal*, September 1933.

[2] Cf. Kirk, *op. cit.* ch. ix. for a thoroughly interesting analysis on these lines.

C

relevance to major cycles; especially in view of the large proportion that agricultural output bears to total output. Yet this is just a variation on the idea of the period of production, an idea the importance of which will be examined later.

2. Is the rate of invention periodic? So far as the subjective activity of scientists goes there is no reason to believe so. There is no regularity. But the conditions favourable to the *commercial exploitation* of inventions are clearly rhythmic. They coincide with the rhythm of the trade cycle itself. They depend on the views held as to the profitability of investments and on the availability of savings. So we should expect that newly discovered utilities and large mass-production schemes will find their proper soil in the upward period of the cycle. Where this involves the introduction of a dominating change in methods of production over a large field, we would expect a considerable effect on the *amplitude* of the trade cycle. Examples are the development of railways, electricity, oil. Yet while Sir Josiah Stamp is correct in hinting that "prosperity is the mother of inventions", and that inventors have to await the flowing tide, still depressions also have their typical inventions, where necessity remains their generator. These inventions will be cost-saving, as against those exploiting an elastic demand or a new utility. But while they are primarily cost-saving, if sufficiently comprehensive they can exert considerable influence on the course

of the trade cycle. Thus some inventions in shipping propulsion have so shortened the period of obsolescence that they have created prosperity in the shipyards: and they may do so again. Such an invention might be quite sufficient to start the upswing of the cycle, if conditions were not unfavourable.

In both cases then we seem to discover rivulets which may play their part in the main stream, without determining its dominant flow. This interpretation supports the view that the trade cycle can be explained only by a systematic logic which properly weights interrelated "causes".

A word on the pure theory involved in these two cases may be added. A bounteous harvest is a gift of nature, and therefore a case of a greater supply at approximately the same cost: or a lowering of working costs per unit. If demand is elastic, an increase in receipts will tend to increase the demand of the favoured industry for the goods of other industries. A bumper harvest may be expected to cause a sudden leap in the demand for agricultural machinery and transport facilities [1]—or the development of oil, a sudden leap in the demand for oil tankers. One cannot too often repeat the simple fact that such a leap may double activity in the capital industries concerned and that once adequate new plant has been produced the relapse in the

[1] Of course a second bumper harvest in succession would probably have very different effects, owing to the notorious limitations of the human stomach. But the example is merely illustrative. The elasticity of the demand for oil would probably be more stable over a longer period in modern circumstances.

plant-producing industries will be equally severe.[1] For it explains why the absolute contraction in the depression stage is concentrated dominantly on the plant-producing industries.

Finally, we may note some facts in the actual structure of industry which we would expect to cause fluctuations of a rhythmic sort in output. Firstly there is the growing proportion of overhead costs in large capitalistic concerns of the modern type. Once capital is so invested it is considerably frozen. It follows that if over-estimates of future demand are made, these oncosts will be very heavy per unit of the necessarily lower output. Such concerns will be faced either with closing down— when they will have to reckon with the large expenses of that course—or with selling at a price which does not cover oncosts. Once plant is in operation, supply costs become fairly rigid.[2] In itself this factor would not explain why all industries expand and contract together. But add the influence of competition. When a just reason for expecting higher profits arises in the development of some pervasive invention, then each competitor will tend to take part in the expansion of plant. The longer the period before the new plant comes into operation, the more likely is over-expansion to occur: for competitors remain in relative ignorance

---

[1] Cf. D. H. Robertson, *Banking Policy and the Price Level*, p. 11.

[2] Plant here of course is a comprehensive term; for instance it includes investment in rubber or coffee plantations and all others of this type, where oncosts are heavy because the period of gestation is lengthy.

of each other's doings; yet meanwhile higher prices due to better, but unfulfilled, expectations continue. Once all the competitors have so invested a situation is inevitable in which the instrumental industries are over-expanded. As each unit has already discounted the elasticity of the demand, and also over-estimated its share of that demand, slump is inevitable. Cut-throat sales or slow reorganisation alike entail prolonged depression, especially if industry is not so constituted that it can cut its losses quickly.

So even apart from the factor of elastic credit there are objective reasons for expecting rhythmical fluctuations in output. Of course without such elasticity, investment would have to depend on voluntary savings,[1] so that the amplitude of the cycle would be diminished greatly. But the great expectations caused by striking inventions would not necessarily be entirely checked by the fall in prices caused by increased saving—savings specifically made to finance them.[2]

[1] Cf. p. 88.

[2] For rates of investment are determined by particular prospects of future profits rather than by present price-levels. And as future prospects are influenced not only by what is reasonable but also by our psychological constitution, the possibility of over-investment is always present, even in these circumstances. The oncosts of such over-investment would accentuate depression.

CHAPTER III

MONETARY

1. THE consideration of monetary influences almost inevitably takes as its text Mr. Hawtrey's conclusion: "The trade cycle is a purely monetary phenomenon". Rhythm in economic activity is a result of inadequate control of bank credit. Mr. Hawtrey does not mean that adequate control would abolish industrial fluctuations: as he insists, the problem of the cycle is simply the *regularity* of its swings. If then he proves that the actual currency system does impose rhythmic fluctuations on economic activity, the only line of criticism left will be that adequate control of credit involves more than monetary control. In that case the cycle could hardly be "purely monetary". It may be that credit control is not a clear-cut function that can be divided off from the prime movers in economic life. In that case, while fully agreeing with the importance ascribed to credit control, we should also have to define the limits of its efficacy; such a definition would then reveal those forces in economic life (if any) which cannot be controlled by the banks, and which therefore may also be causes of the regular swings. Meanwhile we must summarise Mr. Hawtrey's argument under its main headings: (1)

that the regular swings are the result of the inherent instability of credit under modern conditions; (2) that the banking system could cure this instability.

Three of Mr. Hawtrey's definitions must be understood—consumer's income, consumer's out-lay, and the unspent margin. Consumer's income is simply the total of incomes expressed in money. Consumer's outlay is the money total spent out of incomes. It does not therefore include any spending of the proceeds from the sale of a capital asset; nor does it include the expenditure of working capital so far as the source of this expenditure is the sale of commodities by traders (including producers). For this just represents the turning over of a trader's working capital. But consumer's outlay does include any addition to working capital which a trader finances out of his income, just as it in-cludes any new investment made from income. In a word, these two definitions seek to define the original and underived sources of demand. The un-spent margin is the amount of money and bank balances held by consumers and traders.

How, then, does the present type of banking control cause regular successions of expansion and depression? In Mr. Hawtrey's view the character-istics of the trade cycle are, first, a rising then a falling price-level; and secondly, rising then falling productive activity (a description he prefers to fluctuating production[1]). Rising prices and rising

---

[1] *Trade and Credit*, p. 83. This distinction should not be over-stressed. Of course in theory "productive activity" eliminates the

activity occur together, and *vice versa*. Thus the
expansion period responds to an increase in money
demand. In fact the cycle is just a regular rise and
fall in consumer's outlay. The second step is concretely to connect this change in consumer's outlay with industrial activity. The link emphasised
by Mr. Hawtrey is the trader or middleman. Traders
hand on changes or expected changes in consumer's outlay. To meet a growing outlay they try
to replenish their stocks more rapidly than they
sell them—and *vice versa* for a shrinking outlay by
consumers. Now, traders' stocks are financed by
their working capital: this capital they replenish
by sales, when they absorb cash, and diminish by
purchases, when they release cash. So when they
wish to buy stocks more rapidly than they sell—
that is, in the rising cycle—they desire more working capital: in the decline they wish less.

It is worth considering why traders prefer to use
temporary loans rather than personal incomes to
finance changes in their holdings of stocks. The
reason is that a bank overdraft can fluctuate so as
exactly to correspond to the changes in stocks
held. There is no waste. On a trader's income there
are other claims which would conflict with the

influence of the long-period upward trend in production caused by
improved methods. But in practice it is difficult to get an exact
index of productive activity; for employment figures include the
effect of the long-period greater efficiency trend. Perhaps the
most exact description of the actual phenomenon is to say that
while the trend of productivity rises steadily the curve of actual
production fluctuates fairly regularly above and below that
trend.

requirements of business. Also income depends on
the profits made, and these come after the holding
of stocks for which finance is required.

Whence, then, is any new finance to increase
the rate of stock-holding to be drawn? Mr.
Hawtrey says there are two possible sources.
Firstly, traders may intentionally save out of their
incomes. But if they do so, they only change the
direction of consumer's outlay. They do not add to
it. The fall in consumer's outlay on finished goods
will be exactly compensated for by the rise in investment in stocks. As consumer's outlay remains
the same no increase in activity will occur.[1]

Secondly, the new finance may be supplied
through bank loans. As contrasted with savings,
these do create extra consumer's outlay. For
traders can increase their stocks, or release cash,
without needing to reduce their outlay on final
commodities.

The course of the trade cycle can now be summarised. Activity is first stimulated by some extraneous
cause. The increase in demand causes traders to
accelerate their purchases for stock. If they borrow
from the banks to finance this increase, they release
cash. This cash reappears as added income in the
hands of those income earners who co-operate in
the increased production. But with this rise in
consumer's income will be associated a rise in

---

[1] May not diversion from finished to capital goods have ulterior
effects? They will certainly not be great if financed by voluntary
savings: but this point will arise later.

consumer's outlay. So the wheel begins to swing round again—credit is inherently unstable. A rise in the demand of traders leads to increased production, therefore to increased incomes, therefore to increased outlay, therefore to increased demand by traders. At first, says Mr. Hawtrey, there is no occasion for an advance in prices; for producers and traders are making profits through a more rapid turnover. The rise will begin when costs of production begin to rise; and this is inevitable when plant reaches its optimum load, and thereafter diminishing returns emerge. It is worth noting that the rise in profits through increased turnovers will *itself* increase investment, and therefore make this rise in costs inevitable if the expectation of such profits lasts long enough.[1]

It might be asked, would not the rise in prices automatically check consumer's outlay? This would be so if the banks refused to finance the rise. But under existing conditions of central-bank control the banks are not willing to enforce restriction in time. It pays them to lend, and if deposits are growing they wish to lend. The traders on their side wish to borrow to carry stocks so long as a rise in prices is in progress: for the rise itself increases the value of their stocks. So the increase in bank loans will be checked only when the central bank enforces this: that is, when the central bank is becoming nervous about its proportion or about

[1] Compare the difficulties experienced by the Federal Reserve Board in checking speculation in 1929.

weakness in the foreign exchanges resulting from a relative growth in imports. Of course this stage can arrive only after the increase in loans has worked out its effect. Even then forward orders would have to be cleared off, whatever the price of loans. Thus, since the central bank's check comes too late, a vicious upward spiral of productive activity is inevitable.

TURNING PERIOD AND SLUMP.—Central-bank action puts a stop to the growth of credit. Just as before, only in the opposite direction, this entails a fall in the orders of traders. They will begin to absorb cash. Activity will decrease, consumer's income will fall, consumer's outlay will diminish and traders will order still less. Producers will soon be forced to reduce prices. But this very fall makes traders still less willing to hold stocks, now a depreciating asset. So orders will fall off still more. There is a vicious downward spiral.

Why, then, has there been approximate similarity in the length and amplitudes of booms and depressions? Mr. Hawtrey answers that the acceleration of loans takes a fairly definite time to influence central bank's proportions sufficiently for contraction to become necessary. So long as prices do not rise the effect on that proportion would not be serious. Certainly more legal tender would be required—especially for wages. But recipients of income would at first tend to rebuild their savings in cash or deposit balances: for these would presumably be depleted by the previous depression.

Thus demand would not at first increase in proportion to the new purchasing power made available. Also, so long as the price-level does not rise relatively to external levels, imports will not be encouraged: gold will not be lost abroad. Only when industry is working up to capacity will the rise in prices be forced. Loans continue at an accelerating pace. Income receivers are now more willing to spend: the vicious circle accelerates. At this point imports will be encouraged, gold will flow abroad, and here the question of the central bank's proportion will arise.[1] This process will presumably take a fairly similar period to work itself out at different times in an international gold standard system.[2]

The argument seems satisfactory for expansion periods. For slumps it is more difficult. A check to excessive lending will spread through the world. But in slumps, depressed trade lasts longer than the advent of cheap money. That is, however, rather an aspect of the problem, why do slumps last as long as they do? This we shall discuss later. Granted that depression reflects falling or stagnant price-

[1] The fact that if gold flows abroad it must flow somewhere, and so increase the credit basis there, raises this awkward problem for the monetary theory. The trade cycle occurs in all countries more or less at once; yet the fact that the credit basis is strained in one country implies its increase in others. Perhaps the escape from the logical impasse is a practical one: the fact of British control of the flow of world credit before the war, and of American and British "duopoly" after it. On this difficulty see Allyn Young, *Economic Problems*, p. 70.

[2] Compare the shorter cycles of the United States. But there internal monetary factors dominate the situation, and these will work out their effects more quickly.

levels, the periods taken for this fall to reach rock
bottom would be similar in length for the same type
of reason. The difficulty is rather to define rock-
bottom. Mr. Hawtrey says "the process of contraction will eventually be brought to a dead stop when
it comes up against a hard core of unshrinkable
gold".[1] But this seems almost as metaphorical as
"rock-bottom". For after all the value of gold is
itself variable, as recent events in the United States
have shown. Perhaps here we come against other
than "monetary phenomena".[2]

Meanwhile, the two pillars of Mr. Hawtrey's
theory can be defined as follows. (1) Extra bank
credit is essential to an excessive increase in industrial activity. (2) The banks could control that
excessive increase. The trade cycle is due to the fact
that the central banks do not impose the checks on
lending in time. If they did, the cycle would dis-
appear.

Mr. Hawtrey is the pioneer of modern trade-
cycle theory. His central doctrine is now generally
accepted. So far as the harmful excesses of the
swings go, if the banking system acted correctly it
could abolish them. The cure of excessive expansion
would avoid excesses of depression. In this sense
the trade cycle is a monetary phenomenon. These
further difficulties however emerge. First, *can* the
banking system check expansion in time—not only
as at present organised, but even as it might

---

[1] *Trade Depression and the Way Out*, 1931, p. 83; cf. New Edition,
1933, p. 102.   [2] Cf. p. 123.

conceivably be organised? Is enough known about
the sources of excess? And secondly, while this
remains unsolved, there also remains that practical
enigma, the slump. Has it characteristic symptoms
of its own? How can it be shortened as far as is
wisely possible? These questions suggest that some
amplifications are necessary.

2. The question "Can the banks stop excessive
activity in time?" depends for its answer on the
reply to this further question, "Can demand rise
sufficiently to cause excess, without an increase in
the rate of credit creation by banks?" For the
central bank can certainly check the latter rate.
Mr. Hawtrey has always argued on the lines of this
statement: "If credit policy were based on stabilisation of the price-level (suitably interpreted) instead
of on gold reserves, cyclical fluctuations could be
eliminated altogether". That is, regularity would
go, not necessarily fluctuations. This position certainly implies faith in the bank's power to stabilise
the price-level (suitably interpreted!). Yet the present cyclical depression in the United States re-
sulted on a period of stable prices there. Here,
however, we must insert the comment that "relative
inflation" is perfectly compatible with a stable
level of commodity prices.[1] For if there is a rapid
advance in cost-saving methods of production,[2]

[1] "Inflation" in view of its effects in over-expanding output;
"relative" as against the downward movement in money costs.
Cf. Haberler in *Gold and Monetary Stabilisation*, pp. 53-56.
[2] Such as actually occurred in the United States, 1925-29.

and if at the same time the level of such prices is
not reduced, the conclusion follows that the means
of payment must have expanded in exact harmony
with the increase in production. In such circumstances it is inevitable that profits, and therefore
production, will expand.

Mr. Hawtrey indeed argues that there was not
excessive credit creation by the banks.[1] But undoubtedly there was a very rapid increase in consumer's outlay—especially on shares. What was
its financial source? There is agreement on this.
The source was simply the rapid increase in profits
due to a real increase in the efficiency of American
industry. These profits, withheld as reserves, were
reinvested *via* the banks in brokers' loans: borrowed by speculators for a rise (the bulls), they
forced up the price of shares. Meanwhile the banks,
far from extending their loans to brokers, were trying to damp them down by higher rates. Future
earning power was thus anticipated in the prices of
shares. Mr. Hawtrey points out that there was
nothing unsound in this so far as the records of the
concerns reasonably justified the rises. But so far
as a rise in stock prices stimulates new issues unduly—as would normally follow, and certainly did
in Britain in 1928—a new factor arises. For new
issues do mean an expansion of consumer's outlay
—whereas without new issues there can be no such
expansion, since every purchase of an old security
involves a sale. New issues in fact will supply that

[1] *Art of Central Banking*, pp. 49, 50.

jerk to the vicious upward spiral which is so dangerous. Even here, however, Mr. Hawtrey holds that
expansion in new issues was "by no means dispro-
portionate" in the United States between 1926 and
1929.[1] One would like to investigate the quality as
well as the quantity of these new issues before
accepting this conclusion. But Mr. Hawtrey seems
to be leading his readers to the residual explanation
of the American crash—that it was due to the restrictive policy of the Federal Reserve authorities
in 1928 and 1929. Partly through alarm at Wall
Street prices, partly because of London influences,
they restricted credit too harshly and too long.
This of course reflects Mr. Hawtrey's view that the
central banks can control the cycle, and are responsible for its aberrations.

There is, however, one possibility which recent
experience is bringing to the forefront. May not an
excessive expansion of prices be based on increasing
velocity of circulation? Mr. Hawtrey complains
about the vagueness of this term.[2] But velocity can
here be interpreted on Mr. Hawtrey's chosen lines
as the rate at which consumer's outlay takes place.
As he says, consumer's outlay is then simply equal
to the product of velocity and the quantity of cash
(money and bank credit), or velocity multiplied by
the unspent margin. But if we remember that consumer's outlay is the force which the banks must
control if they are to eliminate the trade cycle,

[1] *Art of Central Banking*, p. 65.
[2] *Op. cit.* p. 106.

then this difficulty at once arises. The central bank
can control the quantity of cash; but can it control
the velocity of its circulation?[1] If it cannot, it cannot control consumer's outlay, for instance on new
investments made from income. This argument has
been definitely accepted by an official committee of
the Federal Reserve Board, which published its report in 1931. The committee recommends "that the
reserves required to be carried by each individual
bank be determined . . . secondly, on the basis of
the actual activity of the total volume of deposits
held by the bank, that is, the actual dollar volume
of charges which are made to these accounts". In
sum adequate control must be based on velocity
also.[2]

As against Mr. Hawtrey's rather guarded suggestions that prices on Wall Street did not rise danger-
ously, and that crash would have been avoided
if the banks had behaved more wisely, it seems
more convincing to admit that there was over-
speculation in share prices, and that the sudden
inevitable fall in these prices, sweeping away mar-
gins as it did, was bound to spread depression.
On that line of argument we should find the basis
of the increase in share prices, which Mr. Hawtrey

[1] In theory it can be argued that a central bank can cancel an
increase in velocity by reducing the quantity of credit. But the
facts are that this policy is not a recognised part of the art of
central banking, and that the technique necessary to effectuate it
does not exist.

[2] The Committee refer to "the total volume of deposits"; but
these include consumer's deposits.

D

has difficulty in defining, not only in the quantity of loans from industrialists to stock-brokers; but also in the velocity with which these loans were turned over by their users there. Of course the potential velocity of such dealings is abnormally rapid: as Mr. Hawtrey shows, speculators' profits depend on the rapidity of their turnover. So far as such profits are spent on consumption (including new issues) they will affect the consumer's outlay, with the usual results. This is inflation. For the speculative profits—added spending power— represent nothing but exaggerated hopes. Mr. Hawtrey himself states that "towards the end . . . people . . . were using their resources to back nothing more substantial than a continuance of the good luck which had brought big gains to their neighbours".[1]

If the power of velocity is thus admitted, the argument that consumer's outlay can be increased only if the banks increase credit cannot stand. Of course a check to credit creation would also check velocity. But the real issue is—can the central bank correctly control economic activity so as to avoid excess? And the answer seems to be that it cannot, if it cannot assess the effect of one of the terms in the equation—velocity. The central banks must take velocity into account also, and must control the expansion and contraction of the quantity of cash in relation to velocity, before they can hope to control the trade cycle efficiently. But

[1] *Op. cit.* p. 73.

so far it does not appear that they have the requisite knowledge.

We come then to our second problem. If our central banks cannot be relied on to check expansion at the right time, can they cure slumps more rapidly than has appeared possible in the past? Mr. Hawtrey is definite here. "Personally, I have no doubt that by a low bank rate reinforced by purchases of securities on the part of the central bank it is possible to find an escape from any depression, however severe."[1] He is perhaps slightly less definite in April 1933, when he says he is "confident that a sufficient purchase of securities would overcome any depression, however severe".[2] Of course all he need insist on is that easy money will reduce the length of the slump—and few would disagree. But once a depression has become chronic a new problem is raised, how cure it as rapidly as possible?

There is a clear line of cleavage between the doctors. The surgeons say cut out the excess costs. But the danger is either that the patient will not submit, or that he will die of the operation. We cannot reduce wage rates nowadays to this heroic extent: and even if we could it is doubtful if they could alone catch up with falling price-levels. The physicians prescribe injections to stimulate the drooping price-levels. Among the physicians, however, there is a minor, and not too important

[1] *Trade and Credit*, 1925, p. 113.
[2] *Journal of the Royal Statistical Society*, 1933, p. 456.

cleavage, worth considering because it illustrates Mr.
Hawtrey's point of view. He prefers to pin his faith
to flooding the banks with money. Mr. Keynes
would also have the government initiate investment through public works, in the chronic stage of
the disease. Some of Mr. Hawtrey's objections to
such government enterprise need not be considered
here because they are practical. Of course practical
difficulties may be final at any one time; but this is
a question of immediate facts, not of long-period
policy. His theoretic objection centres in his view
that the funds spent by the government must be
either at the expense of consumer's outlay, in which
case no extra spur to industry would be applied: or
they would be borrowed—created by the central
bank. To this creation there is of course no objection. To raise the inflation bogy, when the fact is
that the patient is almost completely deflated, is
stupid. The only way out of a pit is upward. Only
rising prices can cure an excessive slump in prices.
Achieving equilibrium on the slump level is the
blood-letter's cure. But while both these cures are
reflationary Mr. Hawtrey definitely prefers flooding
the banks to government borrowing. Apart from
the risk of inefficient application through the State
mechanism (a risk which must be admitted), he says
that government investment has to meet the same
obstacles as credit expansion. There seems to be
this difference, however. Government does spend
the money, and once it is initially invested, it cir-
culates. This point links up with the emphasis

previously placed on the importance of the velocity
of circulation. Of course Mr. Hawtrey argues that
if funds are sufficiently pumped into the banks they
will be almost forcibly enlisted as agents insisting
on their clients borrowing. This is true; but bankers
are fairly unanimous that with bursting bins they
cannot find borrowers. The pumped-in funds may
be used only to force up the price of gilt-edged
securities. Certainly this in turn will reduce the rate
of interest in such securities, and therefore establish a fillip to ordinary investment. But this is a
slow process. While it hangs fire there are surplus
funds awaiting investment; and it seems arguable
that the circulation of money could be forced to
influence consumer's outlay more rapidly by a
government which applies sound schemes saved
over from the previous expansion period. Certainly,
if government expenditure on capital schemes is
slackened, the only result can be deflation.[1] If the
object, then, is to cure the slump as rapidly as
possible, are these two policies exclusive alter-
natives? Could they not be helpfully combined?
Government schemes need not compete with the
flooding of the banks if investment is lagging behind
the funds available. But governments must be able

---

[1] The question of the budget is a special one. The service of
loans is of course expensive: but it would be more than met over
the course of the trade cycle by the saving through a more ex-
peditious recovery: and in theory the period of the trade cycle is a
scientific budgetary period, whereas the yearly period is purely
conventional, and unscientific. Still we must admit that the latter
is the touchstone of public confidence.

to adjust their schemes correctly so as not to impede private investment. The argument is perhaps suitably closed with Mr. Hawtrey's own words: "The course of my argument is by no means such as to allow no efficacy at all to a programme of capital outlay as a measure for relieving trade depression. But the advantages offered by it are very limited indeed."[1]

These reflections suggest, firstly, that our banking systems, as at present equipped, are unable properly to control an excessive expansion of consumer's outlay, especially so far as new investment is concerned. And, secondly, that they cannot stimulate recovery as rapidly as is desirable, once the inevitable depression has become chronic. It would appear, then, that we require to know more about the causes and results of excessive investment. What are the conditions and motives which result in excessive investment? How does it affect the structure of industry? What rate of investment is not excessive? These are not just monetary phenomena, though they might be capable of proper control by a monetary authority which thoroughly understood them. In present circumstances they must be investigated.

[1] *Journal of the Royal Statistical Society*, 1933, p. 457.

CHAPTER IV

RATES OF INTEREST

1. BEFORE we proceed to the wider aspects indicated at the close of the last chapter some very interesting developments of the monetary explanation must be considered. British economic science owes these direct contributions to the happy insight which has brought Dr. Hayek to London. Our science has been enriched by this graft on to its main stem of the historic and acutely virile Austrian analysis. Trade-cycle theory has especially benefited.

Dr. Hayek's monetary contributions are contained in his *Monetary Theory and the Trade Cycle*. The first section is taken up with a rather sterile examination of the other trade-cycle theories. The main points of criticism are, firstly, that any one of the three main theories does not in itself offer a self-generating explanation. This is certainly true of the technical and psychological theories, though not clearly true of the savings-investment theory. Secondly, it is argued that the other three theories are non-monetary. But this would be a valid objection only if one of these theories claimed to be the sole explanation of the trade cycle: and this no one of them claims to do. In fact it is little more than an academic exercise to try to understand the present

technical system or the present organisation of
saving and investment in abstraction from the
monetary system. The three have grown in organic
union throughout.[1]

The second line of thought in this section is more
fruitful. It is that the monetary explanation must
not be treated as merely depending on the general
level of prices—up-swing going with rising prices,
and *vice versa*—but that it must be grasped as
working out its inevitable actions and reactions
through the technical structure, through saving and
investment, and through business motives. In sum,
he finds the power unit, the self-generating force of
the pendulum in his "monetary system": but the
swings take place in the actual system, and will
be accentuated by the reactions to monetary conditions of investment or business motive, just as
are those of a pendulum by its physical length.
Thus any complete explanation of actual cycles
must incorporate these other forces which intensify booms and depressions, once credit elasticity has set the swing moving. Most theorists
would agree with this, though many would deny
that the saving-investment theory deals only with
an accentuating influence.

Yet Dr. Hayek does tend to decline into a rather
barren type of mechanical logic which only renders

[1] The translation would in fact represent the situation more
truly if it used "credit system" in place of "monetary system".
For it is the credit element of the money system that is regarded
as the villain of the piece. It is not always too clear just what
"monetary system" covers.

more difficult the systematic combination of the various theories. For instance he argues that "real" interconnections are just consequences of the original monetary influences. But are the motives to achieve security or to get rich quickly—the psychological motives—just consequences of the money system? This criticism should not, however, be taken too seriously. For the clash of rival theories is to a regrettable extent somewhat of a Tweedledum and Tweedledee sham fight attributable to the ineradicable pugnacity even of academic economists. It should be discounted. The problem is rather properly to combine their positive contributions.

2. We turn then to Dr. Hayek's positive theory. Note first very carefully the initial assumptions on which he builds. These are strictly deductive. They are hypotheses to simplify and make possible a clarifying analysis. He starts on the norm of a static society. This is suggested by the fundamental trade-cycle problem—which is, "Why do the forces which would appear to be sufficient to restore equilibrium once it has been disturbed become temporarily ineffective and why do they only come into action again when it is too late?"[1] The forces Dr. Hayek means here are those of the price system. Think then of the system of price equilibria outlined in Marshall's theory of value.[2] Where the

[1] Hayek, *Monetary Theory and the Trade Cycle*, p. 65.

[2] Marshall of course did not develop his theory to the bitter end of the trade cycle; cf. his *Principles*, pp. 619-20.

supply of a commodity is face to face with the demand for it in a perfectly competitive market, it does follow that a price will continuously be fixed at which supply is equal to demand, and at which costs are just recovered at the margin. Over a period of time, then, one would in these circumstances expect that, for instance, a fall in costs would automatically be followed by a fall in price per unit such as would obviate any over-rapid increase in the means of producing the commodity. For if prices were kept too high by some producers, others would capture the market. Similarly, a fortuitous increase in demand would be expected, at the outset, to call forth an increased supply only at a higher real cost, so that the rise in price would equate the marginal utility of this commodity to the other marginal utilities. If one tries to avoid this conclusion by saying that errors can be made, then why should they all be made in the same direction? There must be some influence not present in the static system causing unanimity in error, if error it be. In sum, it is argued that in an economy in which money prices exactly reflect the relative forces of supply and demand in a perfect market, there does not seem to be any reason why the trade cycle should develop, or why goods should be first under-produced, then over-produced over a period of some years.

This applies also, he continues, to the relation between present and future goods, or consumption and investment. For the rate of interest is just the

price of free capital or new savings in the capital
market. If, then, for any reason future goods come
to be more valued than present goods, one would
expect the price for command over future goods,
or new savings, to rise at once in a competitive
market: that is, one would expect the rate of interest to rise: and in these conditions, it would rise
just enough to render unprofitable any investment
which was not based on a true estimation of the
actual relative values of present and future goods.
In other words, the actual market rate of interest
would rise to equality with the now higher real or
equilibrium rate; and this rise in the actual rate
would be adequate to keep the values of present
and future goods in equilibrium, or to prevent the
relative over-production of either; assuming, as
we must without a sufficient reason to the contrary, that everybody is not in error in the same
way at the same time.

This initial assumption of the static self-equi-
librating society is therefore valuable in showing us
where we should look for an explanation. We assume a situation in which money prices exactly
reflect the costs in efforts and sacrifices, as against
efficient desires. But what changes will occur if
we next suppose that money can be spontaneously
created, and acquired by one type of producer, for
instance capital plant producers, to extend their
operations? This of course destroys the perfect
market. The created capital is not drawn from
voluntary savings. It represents no sacrifice-cost

as the static assumption requires. It is an expansion
blown out by the lungs of the banking system. So
far as it is unequally apportioned it would be expected to over-expand some industries, and to
destroy automatic maintenance of equilibrium.

It is on these lines that Dr. Hayek is led to
examine the elasticity of credit in modern banking
systems as the first step to showing how the trade
cycle may be caused. The second step is to see how
this credit is actually applied, and what results are
inevitable when the productive system has suffered
this credit-stimulated alteration.

Having outlined this rather beautiful example
of the deductive method in action, it seems advisable to add some words of warning for the benefit
of those who are unaware of the limitations of that
method of approach. It is, of course, clear that Dr.
Hayek deduces his argument from a basic assumption which, as he would agree, is quite non-
existent. Admittedly, therefore, any conclusions
cannot be regarded as really or actually explanatory
until all the qualifications necessary to transform
the assumed economy into our actual economic
society have been worked out, and fitted into the
final explanation. The danger, inherent in all deductive systems, that actual conditions may be
ignored or never realised, is always present in this
approach.

For instance, in the society of static equilibrium
it is a necessary assumption that men act rationally:
they aim at as profitable business as possible. And

they foresee the working of the price mechanism so
accurately that relative over-expansion of any type
of product cannot be persisted in. The economic
men work a mechanical price-system. The deductive
analysis, beloved of the British classical school,
runs the risks of this unduly mechanical treatment.
Now, while the psychological man of actual life
may legitimately be assumed to be shut out from
the society of static equilibrium, he is certainly in
the very centre of the actual social problem we are
studying. Yet Dr. Hayek indicates that the current
psychological theories must be regarded as external
to the economic situation itself. For they do not
show how mistaken forecasts can all be made together.[1] Well, this may or may not be an adequate
criticism of the actual psychological theories we
have. But, without doubt, the psychology of men's
motives and reactions must figure in any complete
explanation of the cycle. Surely, what we want, for
our future self-expression or for security or in mere
panic, must be internal to this problem. If not, why
bother about it? Why should credit elasticity be
any more "internal" to the economic system than
the prosaic desire to make money as quickly as
possible? In fact the former is rather a result of the
latter. Or again, we assume a static economy: we
see that in it the actual rate of interest would
quickly adjust itself to the equilibrium rate: and
we are then apt to deduce from the obvious fact
that the rate of new savings would be kept equal to

[1] *Op. cit.* pp. 82, 83, 84.

the flow of new investment in such an economy that the saving-investment theory cannot give an internal explanation of the cause of the cycles. In fact, however, one of the strengths of the latter theory is just its grasp of the fact that investment is partly motivated irrationally.

So the risk of exclusiveness in deductive theories must be countered by a determination to fill out the assumptions steadily until they meet the facts. Yet one is apt to feel that for Dr. Hayek the static system tends to be equated to the barter system— the latter being just our system minus the nexus of money and credit. But while you can deduce from the assumptions of barter and economic man, these are certainly not the same as our system minus the credit system. Our system would vanish into thin air without credit. Even the static system is from the first a fiction of the logical imagination. In it there is no credit elasticity, and men are entirely, if materially, rational. Which of these is the more unreal assumption can be left to the reader.[1] Of course these remarks are not meant to shake faith in the usefulness of the deductive approach as a method. As such, the intricacies of the problem make it essential. Also the maintenance of the due balance between inductive and deductive analysis is beyond the wit of man. But constant caution is necessary against accepting strictly deductive

[1] These comments can be compared with the views developed by Allyn Young in *Economic Problems* at p. 201 *et seq.*, where it is argued that "the notion of exchange value is a derivative of the phenomena of *price*".

conclusions as adequate to any actual position in
the trade cycle, before all the facts of the actual
cycle have been digested.

3. Dr. Hayek, then, shows first how a price system in which rational economic men produced and
exchanged in perfect competition would secure the
automatic correction of excess in any type of output. His next step is to use this assumption as a
guide to putting his finger on the influence in the
actual system which upsets the mechanism of the
static system. The outstanding difference is the fact
that our banking systems can expand and contract
credit on their own initiative (credit rather than
money, for money suggests full-bodied value in the
coins, and this would be the type of money which
could not upset equilibria even in a static system,
for it could not be created by the fiat of a bank). So
Dr. Hayek sets out to examine the ways in which
the addition of this partly arbitrary power to vary
credit will alter the working of his stationary
economy: how in fact it will cause self-generating
cyclical movements in output. Remember in passing
that while it is, of course, thoroughly legitimate thus
to add credit elasticity, yet this elasticity is not a
basic economic fact. The urges to self-expression or
to develop the wealth of a society are the inspiration of credit.

The proof that this credit autonomy of the banks
exists can be left over; it is a matter of fact. Let
us first examine the contention that if this credit

elasticity does exist, cyclical fluctuations are bound
to take place. Dr. Hayek's first step takes the form
of attack; it is a negative proof on a limited front.
He shows that a stable price-level has no infallible
power to maintain equilibrium. Recent experience,
especially in the United States, has driven this
home. The wholesale price-level, there and for the
world, remained fairly steady between 1925 and
1929. But this concealed the fact that rapid over-
investment in capital plant was taking place.[1] The
crux of the matter is that when technical progress
is rapid and the price-level is steady, profits will
increase very rapidly through the greater turnovers
made possible by an elastic demand responding to a
decrease in costs: and, of course, growing profits are
the incentive to excessive capital development.[2] In
fact, where output is increasing it is clear that, if
stable prices are to be maintained, the efficiency of
money must increase similarly. But what will be the
effect of this credit increase on the course of investment and saving?

So far as credit is created by the banks to finance
the increased output, it will not be necessary to
increase the rate of interest to the extent necessary
to elicit voluntary savings adequate to finance that
extra output. So at this lower rate of interest the

[1] Cf. p. 36 *supra*.

[2] By profits is here meant the difference between the actual sale
proceeds and the costs borne by enterprisers including their normal
earnings (cf. Keynes's *Treatise on Money*, vol. i. p. 124); or, in
Hayek's sense, profits above equilibrium profits (cf. *op. cit.* pp.
182-3).

rate of new investment will be greater than the rate
of voluntary saving. This simply means that the
actual rate of interest will be kept below the equilibrium rate by the bank creation of credit; meaning
by the equilibrium rate that rate of interest necessary to elicit voluntary savings sufficient to finance
the new demand for future goods. Of course in the
static society, the fall in prices which would be
caused by increased savings would prevent profits
over the normal, and over-investment. But in times
of rapid technical development, it is quite possible
to have continuing over-investment, even with
stable prices, assuming the power to create credit.
For the creation of credit renders extra voluntary
savings unnecessary, and therefore avoids a fall in
prices. And the increase in profits arising from the
more rapid turnovers rendered possible by technical
advances, affords a basis for and an incentive to
over-investment even with stable prices. This then
is quite compatible with the maintenance of stable
wholesale and retail price indices by the banking
authorities during the up-swing of the cycle. The
further actions and reactions will be followed up
later. Meanwhile it should be noted that output
fluctuations are demonstrated to be a surer measure
of the trade cycle than the usual price indices.[1]

The central position of the rate of interest in
this theory should be pondered over. Interest is

[1] Though it may be remarked that the gold standard was not
working according to the vaguely so-called rules of the game in
1925–29.

E

Interest defined

regarded as the measure of the superior valuation put on goods in the present as against goods in the future. The savers require this payment to induce them to save up to the marginal position in the capital market. The investors find it just worth their while to pay for this amount at this rate at the same margin. Interest through time is therefore the measure of the changes in relative value between present and future goods. Its level will control the proportions in which resources are divided between fixed capital, intermediate goods and final goods: and there must be an ideal or equilibrium rate of interest, perhaps visible only to the eye of faith, at which there will be no tendency for resources to be diverted from the production of future to that of present goods, or *vice versa*. Such a rate of interest will in fact divide new savings between the production of future and present goods in such a way that the marginal net products from the two types of investment will be equal in value. In other words this rate of interest maintains equilibrium between the production of future and present goods: and also, therefore, between the amount saved and that spent out of incomes. But if the actual rate of interest can be manipulated by the banking system, over-expansion can be readily explained by this interference in purely competitive pricing. If, for instance, it can be shown that the banks, by their power to create credit out of thin air, can reduce the price of capital below what it is worth, clearly more will be used than if this power

did not exist. So the power of the banks to expand
credit and reduce the cost of investment naturally
links up with the accepted fact that fluctuations in
output concentrate mainly on capital goods. This
subsidy explains their over-expansion satisfactorily
enough.

4. It is next advisable to examine the technical
facts as to the banks' power to expand and contract
credit, and to define the course by which expansion
proceeds to excess and crisis. Mr. Hawtrey has
stated the main trend of monetary events. But
we shall find that Dr. Hayek adds some useful
amplifications and stresses; for instance as to the
inevitability of over-expanded credit, where member banks are autonomous; and as to the inevitability of a lag of the actual behind the equilibrium
rate of interest in such a system. Thereafter, a complete explanation would involve the explanation of
crisis and over-contraction, and especially of the
inevitable self-generation of succeeding over-expansion and over-contraction.

The technical proof of Dr. Hayek's monetary
theory depends on showing that elasticity of credit
is a factor immanent in any system of free enterprise where a central bank is only the central body
in a system of partly independent joint-stock satel-
lites. We have to show how, with our independent
joint-stock banks, it is inevitable that credit
will be increased beyond the amount necessary
to secure that the costs of investment will be

recovered: or, in other words, that during a growth
of trade activity the actual rate of interest will inevitably be kept below the equilibrium rate. The
facts on which this rests are, firstly, the fact that
we have several autonomous competing banks with
the power to increase their loans to producers:
secondly, the fact that the aim of these banks is
to make profit for their shareholders: and thirdly,
the fact that loans advanced originally by one bank
create deposits in other banks, which in turn provide a solid basis for expansion by these other
banks.

The third fact requires demonstration: for it
shows how credit can grow like a rolling snowball,
without disaster, until the central bank steps in the
way. It is the fact made vivid by Mr. Keynes's
description of the banks advancing without dis-
comfort so long as they keep in step.

Suppose the Bank of England acquires £1,000,000
in gold under gold standard conditions. The seller
of the gold will have his deposit with his bank
increased by £1,000,000: and he gives his bank
in return the cheque in his favour by the Bank of
England. Thus his bank will find itself with an
increase of £1,000,000 in its deposit liabilities, and
£1,000,000 in new cash reserves. This bank will
therefore be in a position to, and will normally,
increase its loans. Now if we assume a banking
system (in effect like our own) in which there are
five member banks of approximately equal strength,
the original bank will lose on the average four-

fifths of its new cash at the clearing, as the average proportions of the new loans it has created are gradually paid away to accounts with the other banks. So we can isolate a position in this expanding loan process at which each bank has increased its liabilities by one-fifth of the new cash and each bank has possession of one-fifth of the new cash. Clearly at this position the stage is set for a new expansion of the same kind: the same with this difference, that from this position on there is no need for cash to pass at the clearing, if each bank expands its loans at the same rate. For then the increased liabilities between them will cancel out. So, in fact, the snowball continues to expand until the total new loans granted by all the banks have grown to ten times the amount of new cash.

But will not the member banks' proportions act as an adequate check to excessive expansion of credit, such as occurs in a cyclical boom? Dr. Hayek is especially suggestive when he deals with this argument. He states bluntly that "the key to this problem can only be found in the fact that the ratio of reserves to deposits does not represent a constant magnitude, but, as experience shows, is itself variable".[1] He considers a situation in which the demand for capital has increased—that is, one in which the equilibrium rate of interest has risen.[2] This means, of course, that a greater amount of capital could now be lent at the old or actual rate of interest than could previously. And he points

[1] *Op. cit.* p. 170.　　　　[2] *Op. cit.* p. 168.

out that the member banks will be eager to lend more at the *actual* rate of interest, even if this involves a loss of reserves; for, before the increased demand arrived, they would have had to reduce their rate of interest to lend more. Further, he gives sound explanations of the fact that the actual rate of interest does not rise at once with the new rise in the equilibrium rate. For each bank will feel that if it raises its rate it will just lose its customer to its competitors. In addition to being willing, it is in fact forced by the fact of competition to lend at the existing or actual rate. We thus arrive at the position, just examined, at which one bank begins an expansion of credit and all the others inevitably join in. Finally, Dr. Hayek suggests that where there is an increased demand for capital the risks the banks run by lending are reduced: for losses diminish as the cycle expands: so that the old reserves will provide greater security.

Perhaps one can briefly add some commonplace reasons explaining how credit power can expand in such circumstances. Firstly, there is the factor of the increased velocity of money. So long as this is not taken into account by a banking system in the enforcing of its legal proportions, the explosive power of credit is not under complete control. Secondly, the member banks can vary the proportionate distribution of their assets, so as to effect a reduction in their deposits, or an increase in their cash. Deposits can be decreased, so far as securities are sold by the banks to the public: and in view of the large holdings of securities by banks in times of depression (larger proportionate holdings than the banks desire), this course is liable to be adopted as revival gathers speed. Advances will tend to take the place of securities in the banks' assets, as the revival proceeds. Cash reserves can also be supplemented by a reduction of loans to the money market. If the Bank of England fills the gap, and does not raise its rate, no check to credit expansion takes place.

In sum, perhaps the arguments have sufficed to establish the fact that under present conditions an increase in the creation of credit, once it has been started by an initial increase in demand, can go on indefinitely, so long as the central bank does not disapprove, and so long as the demand for cash from the public does not force the Bank to check the expansion. Dr. Hayek in fact supports Mr. Hawtrey's view that the signal from the central bank comes too late. But he adds analyses of far-reaching suggestiveness. Especially, he explains why the expansion is inevitably accompanied by a lag of the actual rate of interest below the equilibrium rate. If this lag is immanent in the present competitive structure of the banking system, it goes far towards explaining the expansion and crisis portion of the trade-cycle curve. And, as fortuitous increases in demand can be expected to arise at some point in every slump, it helps to explain why slump is bound to develop through recovery into excess once more.

5. At this point a general picture of the process
of expansion will help to define the outline explanation offered by the "Additional Credit Theory of the
Trade Cycle", as Dr. Hayek calls it.[1] The starting
point is that member banks can and, in fact, must
expand credit on the arrival of some fortuitous
factor causing a rise in the demand for capital. This
follows from their competitive nature. Further,
they must so expand credit at a rate of interest
which lags behind the equilibrium rate, the latter
having of course risen owing to the rise in demand.
Thus while the value of future goods has in reality
risen relatively, the price charged for the means of
producing them has not been raised by the banks.
So an artificial stimulus is applied to the expansion
of capital goods. This will continue so long as the
actual rate of interest is below the equilibrium rate,
or so far as demand for capital is met by credit
creation and not by voluntary saving. But, as Mr.
Hawtrey has shown, the time must come when
the reserve ratios of both central and member
banks are threatened by the increased holding of
cash by the public. For this holding will grow
steadily as the credits created percolate gradually
through the expansion of investment into the
pockets of earners. At this point, then, the rate of
the creation of credit must be checked.

It follows that if the rate of new investment is to
be maintained, the only method of filling the gap
caused by the banks is to increase the volume of

[1] *Op. cit.* p. 177.

voluntary saving: and this can be done only by
increasing the actual rate of interest. But this in
turn involves that some of the schemes started on
the basis of the lower interest level will be rendered
uneconomic. For the increase in voluntary savings
will be reflected in a tendency to lower prices for
consumption (or present) goods: and therefore in a
relative rise in the cost of producing capital (or
future) goods. The disequilibrium between the price-
level of present goods and the costs of future goods
is revealed. It needs only the spread of a bankruptcy
epidemic to start crisis and liquidation.

The above seeks to be no more than an outline in the
broad of the contribution which monetary theory,
according to Dr. Hayek, can offer to the problem.
The further filling of the picture must be left to the
next section. But perhaps this sketch can be made
more vivid if it is contrasted with a system in which
there is no possibility of autonomous credit creation.
In the latter, when the demand for capital increases,
the only way in which adequate voluntary savings
can be elicited will be to raise the actual rate of
interest. The actual rate must thus continuously
and automatically coincide with the equilibrium
rate; and any tendency to the excessive production
of future goods will be immediately corrected by
the rise in the cost of producing future goods as
against the value of present goods, in response to
the rise in the rate of interest. At the new actual
(higher) rate of interest only that amount of future
goods will be produced which the lower relative

price of present goods justifies. And this position is a stable one. To put it in another way, any tendency to excessive capital production developing from the increased openings for capital will at once be checked by the increased cost of investment. This society can increase investment only up to the point at which the expected marginal return is equal to the marginal cost of the savings that must be evoked from voluntary savers. As the return falls and the cost rises, a new equilibrium is therefore immediately established at a new rate of interest. It is just Marshall's perfect market.

Contrast this system of automatic equilibrium with actual conditions, in which a lag of the actual behind the equilibrium rate of interest is inherent. In the latter, over-production of capital goods appears as inevitable: and we have established a firm explanation of that relative over-production of future as against present goods which is generally admitted to be the essential ingredient in the vicious trade-cycle expansion phase.

In sum, then, Dr. Hayek demonstrates the effects of elasticity in credit provision by showing how it stultifies the automatic reassertion of equilibrium by an equilibrium rate of interest. Whereas in static conditions a price for capital must emerge which will keep in equilibrium the prices of present and future goods, the autonomous ability to expand (or contract) credit acts like a subsidy (or tariff) on future as against present goods; with this unique characteristic, however, that the subsidy must suddenly be withheld. Then tension or crisis is bound to emerge. When we fill in Mr. Hawtrey's description of the central bank's obligation to call a halt to expansion with Dr. Hayek's analysis, we have a fairly complete diagnosis of the causes of expansion and crisis, and of the need to liquidate the mushroom growths which the crisis exposes. But we cannot yet account for the long-drawn-out nature of depression. Dr. Hayek thoroughly realises this. His explanation is contained in his major and more typical argument. In *Prices and Production* he proceeds to consider the repercussions of this lag in the rise of interest rates during expansions on the structure of real capital. This analysis we must next examine.

CHAPTER V

CAPITAL STRUCTURE

1. In *Prices and Production* it is argued that the excessive creation of credit stimulates an over-development of capitalistic production. Production becomes more roundabout than can be supported by the rate of growth in the prospectiveness or savings of even a steadily progressive community. Thus the equilibrium between the prices of present and future goods is destroyed. Means of producing future goods are artificially cheapened by the lag in the rate of interest, and this leads to their relative over-production. When artificial credit creation ceases and consumers resume their spontaneous rate of saving, the stimulated flow of final goods cannot be profitably sold. This means that there has been an excessive creation of plant, and that labour and intermediate goods have been excessively combined with this plant. The depression cannot end until this lop-sidedness has been corrected; and this must be a slow process. Dr. Hayek says the cure can arrive only through production becoming less capitalistic—less roundabout. This we shall have to examine thoroughly.

At this point we may note that Dr. Hayek is here applying to the explanation of the trade cycle

66

the characteristic doctrine of the classical Austrian school as to the nature of capital. It is therefore interesting to remember that Böhm-Bawerk does not develop the doctrine of roundaboutness within the limits of, or in connection with, the short period. He does not suggest that production becomes less roundabout in short-period depressions; he is not considering the short period. His concern is with the long period. Of course this is not in any sense an argument against Dr. Hayek's assertion that production must become less roundabout if equilibrium is to be restored and depression cured. But it does point to the need to analyse the assertion in relation to the facts.

This doctrine of over-roundaboutness is developed by what we may call the theory of stages in industrial production. Each final good has a period of production from the first investment in its raw material up to its finished state. This period can be regarded as divided into successive stages. At present we may accept the apparatus of these stages as a method of analysis, like a scientist's experimental scaffolding, thinking of them as abstract equal divisions of time. What they may mean concretely we shall consider later. On this assumption we can proceed to examine the phases of the cycle.

2. EXPANSION.—Again we start with the assumption of a society in equilibrium. But here Dr. Hayek emphasises a development of this assumption

—that in this society there are no unused resources. We must remark, by the way, that this is
a condition remote from reality, if we are considering an actual society in time of depression; and that
to complete the investigation the assumptions must
be removed until the facts take their place; and the
deductions from these removals must be drawn.
Dr. Hayek's justification of his method is that we
must assume an absence of unused resources if
we are to assume a static equilibrium, for idle
capacity would entail disequilibrium: in the static
economy they would not be produced. The automatic price system sees to that. And he rightly
insists that we must build on the static hypothesis.
In sum, if we grafted idle capacity on to the
original assumption—the static system—we would
be building on a contradiction. We must either
assume that there are no unused resources or we
must deny ourselves the aid of static economic
reasoning: and that really means the denial to the
economist of his most fruitful method.

We begin, then, on the position, described in
Monetary Theory and the Trade Cycle, in which,
owing to credit creation, the actual rate of interest
lags behind the equilibrium rate. In such circumstances it is possible to extend the roundaboutness
of production—or to lengthen the period of production. This can be vividly, if perhaps inexactly,
explained if one thinks of what a rate of interest
means. A rate of 4 per cent. can be otherwise expressed by saying that an annuity of £4 costs £100:

and this is just the same as saying that the price
of any annual sum is 25 years' purchase (4 × 25).
Similarly, at 5 per cent. the price of an annual sum
is 20 years' purchase. The change involved, then,
by a rise from 4 per cent. to 5 per cent. simply
means that the period for which lenders are prepared to wait for the return of their capital has
fallen from 25 to 20 years. This in turn means that
in these circumstances borrowers should recover
borrowed capital in 20 as against 25 years. In
other words, when the rate of interest rises they
must shorten their period of repayment, or increase
their rate of depreciation, and *vice versa*. Dr.
Hayek therefore argues that when the equilibrium
interest-rate rises the equilibrium period of production shrinks, and *vice versa*. In fact, with the
lag of the actual behind the equilibrium rate of
interest, the period of production is expanded too
rapidly, and has to be painfully and too slowly
diminished in the slump. I have some difficulty in
interpreting the meaning of Dr. Hayek's last step
as to the contraction of the period of production—
but this will be discussed later.[1]

Granted, then, that a fall in the actual rate of
interest will cause an increase in the investment of
capital, which, being able to look further ahead,
can become more roundabout: it follows that if the

---

[1] It may, however, be remarked that the fact that the period of
production is too long to permit of prosperity *relative to slump conditions* does not necessarily involve a change in technical methods.
It only involves writing down the capital value of concerns, by
liquidation if necessary, and so reducing costs.

actual rate at any time lags behind the equilibrium rate production will become too roundabout for equilibrium to be maintained. Resources will tend to flow more towards those stages of production nearer the beginnings of the productive process, and away from those stages nearer the finished product. This is the only way in which investment for the future can be increased. In practice the division of labour will be pushed further; new or more specialised methods, like electric welding, will be developed; or larger plant suitable for a greater turnover will be laid down. These changes can be effected only by increasing the flow of intermediate goods—labour power and materials— towards the initial stages of production; and diminishing the flow previously employed in the stages nearer the outflow into consumption. This *transfer* is inevitable if we assume there are no unused resources. Now, as Dr. Hayek points out, credit creation, resulting in a lag in the actual rate, will bring about this transfer through an appropriate change in the relative price-levels of future as against present goods. When producers are provided with credits their demand will increase relatively, and they will draw factors of production towards the creation of capital plant: this will increase roundaboutness because at the lagging rate of interest the increase is profitable. Similarly, forced saving[1] will render the production of final

---

[1] That is, saving imposed by a rise in prices on those whose incomes do not expand proportionately with the rise in prices.

goods relatively less profitable. Thus as long as the
rate of credit creation continues, the production of
more roundabout plant will continue. And when
credit creation slackens or stops the economic
system will be saddled with plant which depends
for its profitable working on the continuance of an
artificially lowered rate of interest. To revert to
our former example of an actual rate of 4 per cent.
when 5 per cent. is the equilibrium rate; the plant
has been constructed on the basis of its capability
to recover its capital value in 25 years. It can not
be profitable if 20 years is all the prospectiveness
the equilibrium rate of interest will justify. When
credit creation ceases, and the actual rate rises to,
or above, the equilibrium rate, this situation will
be unmasked.

3. THE PEAK TURNING PERIOD.—We have rein-
terpreted the monetary reasons for the turn in the
production curve. We have now to re-state this
argument in terms of real capital developments.
Remember that in a static economy a rate of interest simply measures the discount on future as
against present goods. At that rate the values of
future and present goods are held in equilibrium.
If, by credit creation, the rate is actually lowered
below the equilibrium rate, the production of future
goods will be excessively stimulated. If this support
is suddenly withdrawn, we must expect that the
natural demand for future as against present
goods, which existed before the credit creation, will

F

reassert itself. Assuming the static society then, when the artificial credit inflow stops, the demand for future goods relative to present goods will fall. Labour and materials will be diverted from the lower stages to the stages nearer the final commodity—either to this or to idleness. If we assume that there are no unused resources (a legitimate assumption at the peak), this will mean that the more elaborate plant which sprang up in the expansion period will be bereft of its necessary supply of intermediate goods. So far as this happens, it will be forced to close down; or will have to undertake liquidation of capital charges, if it tries to pay the increased cost of attracting its necessary material.

One can put this another way. We start with the static economy. In it there is a certain prospectiveness determined by the extent to which people are prepared to sacrifice the present to the future. It is measured by the equilibrium rate of interest. If credit is created, this balance, which is based on actual economic preference, is upset. The injection makes it worth while to produce for a more distant future, and imposes abstinence on consumers. If the credit creation suddenly stops, we should expect that, with the consequent fall in prices, the old level of prospectiveness will reassert itself. The demand for present goods will resume its former relative strength; and those investments which depended on an artificially increased demand for future goods will be revealed as unprofitable. For people are not

voluntarily willing to save as much as these more
roundabout methods require for profitable working
over the longer period of production.

These arguments do help us to understand why
the depression is such a long and painful proceeding.
If it be true that in depression the excessive roundaboutness of actual productive methods must be
corrected, and that less roundabout methods must
be substituted, one can in fact be pardoned for
wondering how recovery can ever take place. For
roundaboutness seems to depend on technical
arrangements in industry. A reorganisation of these
would require so many surgical operations that the
death of the patient seems more likely than his
convalescence. However this criticism's justification depends on the interpretation which is placed
on the doctrine of stages; to which we shall turn in
a moment.

Meanwhile, we may remark on the Spartan treat-
ment, which follows from Dr. Hayek's analysis, as
the only road to cure. Clearly a recrudescence of
producer's credits will only restart the vicious
circle.[1] So long as excessive roundaboutness exists
they can only serve to support and expand the
excess. The sole remedy is to bring the level of
roundaboutness once again into harmony with the
rate at which people are prepared to save voluntarily. It would seem that this can be achieved only

[1] The argument that an increase in consumers' credits will also
cause disequilibrium will be found in *Prices and Production*, p. 81
et seq.

by a reduction in costs and a painful process of
liquidation, until the time arrives when a sufficient
turnover can be produced from the existing plant
and sold at a remunerative though lower price. No
wonder the time is long, the way painful. But even
this latter interpretation is probably a gloss on
Dr. Hayek. It depends, once again, on how the
theory of stages is understood. So much then for
exposition. We turn to a more critical examination.

The essence of Dr. Hayek's theory is the application of the Austrian theory of the function of
capital to explain the trade cycle. Böhm-Bawerk
shows how an increased flow of real resources towards the more remote stages of production is
necessary if the system is to provide more adequately
for the future.[1] This diversion implies that people
are more willing to defer their consumption than
they were before it took place. The doctrine is
thoroughly convincing if we are trying to understand how capitalist production develops over the
long period: for over that period it implies also that
the present will be steadily more fully provided for
as previous investments fructify. We can also see
that this more capitalist production can and does
develop too rapidly in the boom of the short period.
But the idea that production becomes *less* roundabout in the short period, that the number of stages
decreases, is more strange to us. Yet we must construct a clear picture of what this can actually

[1] *Positive Theory of Capital*, ch. ii. (Smart's translation).

mean, if Dr. Hayck's theory is to become distinct,
and is not to remain vague.

4. INTERPRETATION OF STAGES IDEA.—The first
natural interpretation is that division of labour or
the *technical* stages of production increase in booms
and decrease in depressions. This is the "natural"
view because in economic development, as Böhm-
Bawerk shows, this development of specialisation
is just a technical *fact* of history, to be accepted as
such. "The fact that a greater product is obtained
by methods of production that begin far back is
essentially a purely technical fact, and to explain
questions of technique does not fall within the
economist's sphere."[1] Greater roundaboutness
simply means greater specialisation—at least this
is its most significant meaning in the long period.
But we must face up to this question: do the *technical* stages of production decrease, like the curve
of a folded fan, in depressions. So put, the question
must be answered in the negative. As a general rule,
technical specialisation is not reduced. In depressions we do not find that more efficient methods of
production, more efficient machines, are replaced by
less efficient methods and machines. The development of the application of electricity to industry
grows steadily even in these bad years, though it
grows more slowly. What we do hear of is liquidation. Capital is written down, or plant is sold up,
until money costs are sufficiently reduced to make

[1] *Op. cit.* p. 20.

the working of the same plant profitable. During this process much plant will have to remain unused or only partially used. And at the same time the relative increase of savings will be tending to pull down the actual rate of interest towards the lower equilibrium rate. This is one road to recovery among others. Also a stimulus is given to cost-saving inventions, rather than to inventions creating new utilities, which are more germane to the expansion periods. The period of depression is just the period in which this liquidation is with difficulty proceeding. For men admit losses unwillingly, especially if creditors and debtors are of different nationalities. Until liquidation is accomplished, however, the effects of the over-rapid expansion of plant continue to operate: it cannot then be profitably worked in view of its money costs and of the money demand for its products. So we must conclude that the technical steps in production are not reduced in slumps. In fact, surely the costs of this type of reduction would be quite prohibitive; for the whole organisation of raw materials and labour have been fitted into the previous scheme.

It is not, of course, denied that adaptations to a fall in demand during depressions may take the form of a reduction in the division of labour. For instance, some employees may be dismissed, and those remaining may have to undertake more varied, less specialised work. What is denied is that there is any *general* reversion to less efficient technical methods as the depression proceeds, and that depressions can be cured only by such a reversion. In fact, firms do not as a rule *replace* their existing plant by less efficient processes. Over-capitalised firms may, of course, go out of business altogether, or may close down the less remunerative branches of their trade; and many of them carry on during a slump without recovering their total costs. But the cure to this situation on the supply side, both in theory and in fact, is a reduction in money costs, partly by necessary liquidation, partly by greater productive efficiency—not a reversion to less efficient technical methods. It is against the latter interpretation of the stages idea that the present argument is directed.

There is, however, a different line of exposition, which is not perhaps too clearly distinguishable in *Prices and Production* from the possibility of elasticity in technical stages. Dr. Hayek also shows that in expansions the average period of production per unit of goods expands, in depressions it contracts. We can take as our norm a community which relies for its capitalist development only on voluntary savings. In that case the flow of intermediate goods to the various stages of production will be determined by the actual relative preferences (or price-levels) for present goods as against goods maturing in the future. In other words, the length of the average period taken by a unit of commodity to traverse the stages between first investment and final sale will be determined by the extent to which people are actually prepared to defer present to future consumption, or are prepared to save. The length of the future period for which they are prepared to save to-day determines that of the period of production: and also secures that the goods will sell at their equilibrium prices as they emerge from the production process. Thus, in a developing community held in continuous equilibrium, the flow of resources to each stage will be regulated by the equilibrium rate of interest, which is also actual. But if in actual expansions the rate of interest is kept artificially below the equilibrium rate the flow of resources towards the lower stages of the production period will be increased relative to the flow towards the more final stages. And it is easy to see that this involves a lengthening of the average time taken by a unit of commodity to pass from its origin to its apotheosis. There will be more goods in a less finished state and less goods in a more finished state. So on the average each unit must take longer to achieve completion. Similarly, if in depression the actual rate of interest tends to be above the equilibrium rate the flow of resources to the more remote processes of production will be reduced relative to that to the stages nearer consumption. And the time taken by each unit to traverse the process will be reduced.

Now, this is just the line of thought which Dr. Hayek is developing when he shows that, when credit expansion is proceeding, non-specific goods will move from the more final stages to the more remote stages; and *vice versa* when the actual rate

of interest rises above the equilibrium rate. This
process is quite reconcilable with the view we have
advocated that the actual *technical* stages do not
contract with depressions. All it means is that in
expansion the turnover of the stages nearer the
raw material will increase relatively, in depressions
it will fall off. And this is also in harmony with the
accepted fact that the output of the capital industries develops over the long period by a series of ups
and downs, the trend being upward; whereas the output of consumption-goods proceeds by a series of
steps; first expansion, then a fairly level output
during depressions.

How then does the explanation of the trade cycle
take shape if we consider inadequate the suggestion
that the technical stages of production increase
then decrease: and interpret it through the view
that in expansion the average period of production
grows, whereas in depressions it contracts? We will
then hold that the very rigidity of the technical
stages is one of the main causes of our troubles.
We cannot go back to less efficient technical stages.
If we could suddenly do so we could certainly cure
unemployment. But the cost would be quite prohibitive. It would be reflected in the standard of life.
The only alternative is to recreate conditions in
which the existing plant can pay its way.

We shall therefore interpret the elasticity of
stages doctrine as meaning a period of production
which at first exaggerates, later inevitably under-
estimates the natural prospectiveness of a society.

Instead of postulating varying technical stages we shall reckon with the fact that, through credit expansion, expectations grow, and plant is created to cope with these artificially increased turnovers. When the credit support is withdrawn, the flow of resources to the lower stages of production slumps suddenly. The turnover of the output of new plant is disastrously reduced. Any new plant produced represents, be it noted, the turnover of a lower stage of production. It is therefore revealed that the scope of plant has outgrown the demand at which its output can be profitably sold: it has outgrown the equilibrium demand, and still more the slump demand, weakened by losses in the capital industries. Oncosts per unit at the expansion capitalisation are too high. The only remedy is reduction of cost per unit by cost-saving invention, or by writing down capital. This must proceed at least until the equilibrium demand for future goods can be economically met. The primary phase of trade depression will then be a period of necessary liquidation; necessary reduction of costs until adequate turnovers can be economically produced from the existing plant at the price which actual unsubsidised demand determines. This need for financial liquidation and for the adequate supply of cost-saving reorganisation is a sufficient positive ground for the long and painful nature of slumps; without also positing the need for almost impossible surgical operations such as the reduction in technical stages would involve.

It is not of course suggested that anything has been added to Dr. Hayek's exposition. The difficulty is rather that he seems to suggest both interpretations of the stages at different times.[1] The interpretation adopted here is that Dr. Hayek means by his elasticity of productive stages simply a change in the relative flows of resources—the relative *amounts* applied—between lower and higher stages of production—or more simply, a change in the average production period, in expansions above, in slumps below the equilibrium production period.[2] On this interpretation the doctrine of stages is merely an abstract division of the process of production, which is convenient for expository purposes. The equal stages of the famous diagram[3] are apt to give one the impression, so prone are diagrams to misinterpretation, that technical stages are meant. Yet there is one reason for insisting on its inadequacy. For is it not likely that the drastic, almost grim, view of the cure for over-expansion taken by Dr. Hayek is partly influenced by the failure completely to dismiss the assumption that technical stages must be reduced in periods of slump?

It may here be remarked that Böhm-Bawerk

[1] Compare *Prices and Production*, pp. 82, 83, and the definition of the "over-shortened process" with the account in "The Paradox of Saving", *Economica*, May 1931, p. 152.

[2] Quotations supporting this view can be found at *Prices and Production*, p. 66; "Paradox of Saving", pp. 147, 152, 155. In fact our statement only reproduces these.

[3] *Prices and Production*, Lecture II.

quite definitely conceives of his stages as technically determined. "Every lengthening of the roundabout process is accompanied by a further increase in the technical result."[1] He uses the idea of stages constantly in his famous chapters on the functions of capital.[2] But while "stages and degrees in capital" are for him technical, they are also long-period factors; and he does not suggest that technical stages ever decrease in fact, though he makes this avowedly abstract assumption for purposes of argument.[3] What may decrease is the relative volume of investment at the lower stages of capitalist production. This quotation, though long, admirably summarises his doctrine. "The length or the shortness of the process, its extension or its curtailment, is not to be measured by the absolute duration of the period that lies between the expenditure of the first atom of labour and the last—otherwise the cracking of nuts with a hammer which might chance to be made of iron brought from a mine opened by the Romans would perhaps be the most 'capitalistic' kind of production. Nor is it to be measured by the number of independent intermediate members which the production process embraces—otherwise when, by means of the three intermediate products, twig, lime, and bird-lime, a boy catches birds on the same day as he commences making these three forms of capital, his

[1] *Op. cit.* p. 84; cp. p. 75 *supra.*
[2] *Positive Theory of Capital,* Books I. and II.
[3] Cf. *op. cit.* p. 111. The article in the *Quarterly Journal of Economics,* January 1896, will also be found interesting.

bird-catching would be more capitalistic than the far-back labour of the miner who devotes years to the sinking of a shaft. But it is to be measured by the average period which lies between the successive expenditure in labour and uses of land and the obtaining of the final good."[1]

The point may have been laboured. But emphasis has seemed necessary, because it helps to explain the sharp cleavage between Dr. Hayek and Mr. Keynes as to the proper remedy for depression. In Dr. Hayek's view we must just wait until bitter experience and inventiveness have reduced costs sufficiently to restore equilibrium: certainly a long process if it involves a regression to less efficient technical methods. He does not appear to envisage a secondary phase of coma, for which much evidence can be found. Therefore he gives no support to policies of stimulated investment in this stage, as Mr. Keynes does. Increased credits, either to producers or consumers, can only increase disequilibrium so long as the enlarged capital industries cannot produce economically. But is there not a secondary phase of depression when output is subnormal not just because liquidation has not proceeded far enough, but because demand is subnormal owing to the effect of the liquidation process on the prospects for new investment? This possibility will be examined when Mr. Keynes's views are considered. But it is worth adding that if this secondary phase is established, we must remove one

[1] *Op. cit.* p. 90.

of Dr. Hayek's assumptions if we are to explain the facts. For at this period of the cycle there is no lack of unused resources: though the assumption is valid enough at the height of the cycle. And unused resources imply inadequate demand, relative to the full working of existing plant, and to adequate prospects for future investment.

5. Perhaps clarity may be served by an attempt to define the distinction between the two successive phases of depression. Dr. Hayek shows admirably the necessity for liquidation: and this process may be taken as the characteristic of the first phase. But no depression will be cured by mere liquidation. It is also essential that new investment should return to equilibrium with current voluntary savings. But does not the very process of liquidation itself produce economic conditions in which it is excessively difficult to re-establish this necessary equilibrium between current savings and new investment? Consider the conditions that develop in the first phase. The losses made in the lower stages of production will cause the demand for capital to fall below the supply: the average period of production will diminish below its equilibrium length: voluntary savings will harden into bank balances: their social uses will evaporate in a lowered velocity, or if they take the form of company reserves, in financing losses. The slump in the demand for capital will have caused the actual rate of interest to rise above the equilibrium rate suitable to the new conditions.

Price-levels, in view of the excess of saving over new investment, will be falling. And there will be no lack of unemployed resources. Without mention as yet of the dynamic of psychology, are not these conditions definitely antagonistic to the emergence of that new investment which alone can take up current savings, and which alone can perform the social service of employing social resources? At this stage there is no question of the more final stages of production stealing non-specific goods from the primary stages: for free resources are there.

It therefore appears that there is a point in depressions at which some stimulus to new investment is socially desirable. Of course there is the obvious practical dilemma. Liquidation of excessive costs must proceed sufficiently, yet new investment must be stimulated. How can you stimulate the new investment, and yet avoid checking the liquidation before it has gone as far as it must? Still, this practical dilemma does not obviate the theoretical necessity to distinguish the two phases of slumps. For if we just wait until costs of production from existing plant are sufficiently reduced to recreate profits, we are ignoring one of the most hopeful lines of escape. Everyone wishes to reduce the length of slumps as much as possible. This is really the correct way to put the problem. Therefore we wish to stimulate profitable new investment, to employ unused resources, as soon as safety permits: for unemployed resources represent inadequate demand. Certainly, if we sit down to

continuous liquidation only, the patient will die in
our hands. For, apart from new methods and investment, continuous cost reduction, which takes the
form of liquidation only, simply means continually
falling demand—a vicious circle indeed. The cure
must come by way of new investment in working
capital and plant: so long as it does not bolster
up positions requiring liquidation, the sooner it
comes the better.

So perhaps we may tentatively suggest two stages
in depressions as we know them: the first one of
necessary liquidation; the second one of excessive
liquidation, a stage which will be long or short
according as the resiliency of the system is sluggish
or rapid, and is hindered or helped by the monetary
authorities.

There can be no doubt that Dr. Hayek digs to
the roots of the real causes of expansions and
slumps. He picks the curve out in red in the structure of industry. He establishes the necessity for
liquidation; no mere monetary policy will solve
structural evils. But he hardly removes all his
assumptions. We are therefore inclined to ask this
question. Should you treat a situation in which
there are unemployed resources, in which the actual
rate of interest is greater than the equilibrium rate,
in which enterprise is abnormally depressed, and in
which necessary liquidation, escaping control, has
become a chronic downward spiral, in the same way
as you would a position in which controlled liquidation to a lower level is clearly necessary? The fact,

however, that the "unused resources" assumption is not removed, quite logically prevents Dr. Hayek from considering the actual disease in depressions and prescribing the cure, as firmly as he otherwise would.

CHAPTER VI

THE NATURE OF SAVING AND INVESTMENT

1. THE nature of saving is best understood by
stages. When we talk of saving we normally mean
something voluntary. This meaning we shall retain
when we talk simply of saving. We receive a certain
income in a certain period. If we refrain from spending all of it, we save voluntarily. We can assume
provisionally that the price-level of final goods
remains stable; then, the value of our savings in
any period will equal the value of our incomes less
the value of our expenditures in that period. This
is the common-sense conception of saving: we shall
see that it is too simple. Having thus retained a
sum of money, the question arises—what to do
with it? The obvious course is to invest it; and from
the holder's point of view the normal course is to
build up a balance or bank account; and when sufficient has been there secured, to turn the surplus
over what is required in this liquid form into some
security. Deposit receipts may be regarded as a
transitional cistern replenishing either liquid balances or the more permanent holding of securities.
There is then a regulated amount held as bank
balances, or ready money. This latter fund also
finds its way into investment through the action
of the banks in lending their deposits.

From this account it appears that we have the convenient habit of holding a certain amount of our income in the form of ready money. From the individual point of view this money is a hoarding. Its amount depends on what sum we find it convenient to hold as purchasing power. But in some conditions of trade a desire to hold money rather than to invest savings in goods or securities may become prevalent. In this case we would say that the *community* had evinced a propensity to hoard; in addition to the purely provisional act of saving it has expressed a preference for hoarding, or holding money, over investing money saved. It is this communal preference for hoarding that has important effects on the course of the trade cycle. A glance at the trend of bank balances (including saving deposits) as against that of new investment in a slump will prove the existence of this preference, and of its opposite in a boom. This is something additional to mere saving, which is just a "negative" act, just the refraining from spending. Hoarding is a positive decision as to how to use the surplus, just as is investment. It may of course be said, Cannot the banks defeat the hoarding propensity, so far as money placed with them goes, by increasing their loans? That may or may not be so. But even if it is so, the fact remains that there is a preference to defeat. There is the fact that the community on balance wishes to hold money rather than goods or shares. This is hoarding.

So far, the price-level has been assumed stable,

and saving has been examined from the individual point of view. But if everybody increases the proportion of incomes saved together, clearly demand for final goods must fall, assuming the level of production and the efficiency of money do not alter.[1] So the price-level must fall proportionately, and everybody will be able to buy the same amount of goods and services as before with a smaller money outlay, the balance in money representing increased savings. This almost looks as if the problem of producing something out of nothing had been solved. But the miracle is, as usual, a delusion—and a snare. Everybody has set out to save more in money: and this unanimity has achieved the money saving, and yet avoided any saving in the consumption of the community's goods. It would be truer, however, to say that nothing has been produced out of something. For the money savings that have accrued to the savers without any sacrifice of consumption must have been drawn away from some other function in the economic system. They have in fact been drawn off from enterprisers. For if the latter were just recovering their costs of production (including normal earnings of management) before the saving bacillus became active, then with the fall in prices and their costs unchanged they will be making losses. And their losses imply the start of Mr. Hawtrey's vicious

---

[1] The first effect of increased saving will be an increase in traders' stocks. The fall in prices will then follow. In the opposite case (p. 91) traders' stocks will first diminish.

downward spiral. So if the savings are merely hoarded, and the banks cannot engineer compensation for this hoarding, the increased consumption which lower prices will bring must be accompanied by decreased production. We may truly say in these circumstances that consumption has become less productive, or less reproductive than it was. This general argument would hold in all cases in which the rate of hoarding increased. For while an increase in the consumption of final goods may at once be expected, owing to the fall in prices, this increase could not be sufficient to prevent losses to producers, assuming initial equilibrium conditions. To prevent such losses the expansion in consumption resulting from an elastic demand would need to be sufficient to compensate exactly for the fall in producers' money receipts: that is, consumers would need to spend as much money as before; and this contradicts the assumption that hoarding has increased. Assuming initial equilibrium then, increased hoarding imposes either losses on enterprisers, which will react on their outlays; or lower rewards to the factors of production, which will also diminish demand.

So much for the effects of a falling price-level: while consumers who are prepared to spend as much money as before will get a windfall in real goods, if excessive saving is occurring, consumers' money outlay as a whole must diminish. Where the price-level rises, for instance through a relative rise in the activity of money, analogous reactions

take place. Such a rise means that if consumers
continue to spend the same amount in terms of
money, then they will draw to themselves a smaller
proportion of the community's real income. If we
think of that care-free individual, the man who
spends all his income, then we see that a rise in
prices will force him to be content with less real
consumption. It is, however, likely that the value of
this man's contribution to the community has itself
risen with the rise in prices, though his salary or
wages may lag behind. In this case our individual
is really being forced to save for and by the community. For he has to consume less: and he is
giving as much as before in real terms to the community. Mr. Robertson's term, "automatic lacking", is therefore exactly descriptive of our example's unfortunate plight. So far as he is concerned, the circumstances are automatic: like the
young lions of the psalmist he must "lack and suffer
hunger". From the individual point of view, then,
automatic lacking is a correct companion for
voluntary saving. But when we look at it from the
community's point of view perhaps forced saving
is the more suitable term. When consumers are thus
forced to spend less, the real goods they are denied
of course become available for those who can pay
the higher prices. But these luckier individuals will
be those who control the new funds that have been
created: the new borrowers the banks have
favoured, or perhaps the consumers given credits
on the instalments system. In fact, therefore, one

section of the community has been enabled to draw
off an increased flow of real goods from the communal stream, and the others have been forced to
cut down the share they formerly chose. In this
way our war governments diverted resources into
the production of war materials, and forced those
gaining no equivalent advantage from war activities to do with less. In view of the fact that the
meaning of saving is more established, forced saving seems a more suitable term than automatic
lacking, for the purposes of this introductory
summary.

2. This analysis indicates a further step. Most
people divide their incomes into two portions, one
of which they save, and one which they spend. So
far as they are practical economists they will of
course strike the balance where the marginal
utilities from the portions saved and spent are
equal. Let us think, then, of an income of £500 a
year, £400 of which is spent and £100 saved. If we
next assume a rise in the price-level, the £400 to be
spent will be worth less in goods. Our spender is
faced with a dilemma. If he cannot bring himself to
any sacrifice of the real present, he will stabilise his
expenditure in goods; and his money savings will
fall off, which means that his real savings will fall
off still more. If his faith in saving is fanatic, he will
maintain the real value of his savings, and his real
spendings must fall off more than in proportion to
the rise in prices. But these are the unlikely and

limiting extremes. Most of us compromise. The marginal utilities will tend to be equalised higher up the utility scales of saving or spending for each spender. The usual compromise will probably be that rather less real income will be consumed by those whose money-incomes do not rise proportionately to the rise in prices. Not only will higher prices cause a direct and automatic decrease in real consumption, but the desire to support the value of the proportion saved in terms of goods will cause some further decrease in real consumption. For with the rise in prices some consumers at least will notice that the real value of their saved money proportion has fallen. Here again, then, some goods are released for other uses. Mr. Robertson calls this further increment to saving induced lacking—induced, because a mixture of necessity and intelligent reaction to necessity has been operative.

There will, however, also be present a tendency limiting the importance of induced saving, as we shall call it. For the comfortable incomes there exists a considerable margin of savings, some of which may correctly be described as automatic. In these cases the marginal utility of savings is very low. If, then, these incomes rise less than proportionately to a rise in prices, it is likely that the level of customary expenditure will be supported by their holders at the expense of reducing the money proportion saved. In this case there can be no release of resources for use elsewhere. In fact, this seems the more likely course to be taken by *rentier* incomes

in periods of expansion. For this reason it is perhaps
sufficient for our purposes to carry with us the idea
of forced savings only. The importance of forced
savings is not of course diminished by what has
just been said. For the bulk of consumers have not
the comfortable margin involved. And even the
whole class of those who have such a margin will
consume somewhat less, other things remaining
equal. When prices rise faster than wage incomes,
the lag will force their earners to consume less than
the value of their product. It seems unlikely that
wage-earners will proceed to spend less than they
would have otherwise, specifically to build up
money balances. Of course they may build up
money balances nevertheless; but this because their
absolute earnings will increase. The point is that
they will not spend less *in order to* build up money
balances—that is, they will not be *induced* to save.
Induced saving seems therefore to be confined to
the income range of the medium and the very
worthy: and, on purely economic grounds, perhaps
here we may ignore them.

3. A summary of these distinctions may now be
helpful. There seems to be this logical progress in
the process of saving.

(1) Voluntary saving is simply spending less than
one's income. The *absolute* proportion so saved
may of course grow or diminish simply because of increased or diminished capacity to
save or because of higher or lower interest

rates in booms or depressions respectively.
The variations are still voluntary.

(2) Forced saving is the necessity, following on a
rise in the price-level, to consume still less
than in (1), because the money proportion
previously spent has diminished in value.
This will entail saving for the community so
far as the decrease in the saver's consumption
is not more than offset by a fall in the value
of his output. But the natural situation will
be that the saver's output will increase proportionately with any increase in the price-
level. Where the saving margin is comfortable
it is probable that a somewhat increased proportion of the income will be spent. But the
amount of real goods consumed will also fall
off somewhat, and this will entail real saving
for the community.

(3) Induced saving arises out of Stage (2) if it is
noticed that the money proportion saved has
decreased in real value, and if consumption is
further cut down to restore the real proportion previously saved.

On the same lines it follows that a fall in prices
and a lag in the fall in incomes will result in some
increase in real consumption, together with the
probability of some increase in the money proportion of incomes saved. A further increase in real
consumption might be induced by the realisation
that the money proportion saved has increased in
real value through the fall in prices. But it is safe
to say that the great mass of the saving faithful is
innocent of such economic introspection. In view of

our prevailing money psychology it is likely that in these circumstances savers will tend to re-establish the money proportion they regard as wise, which will have been infringed during the boom. This will tend to mitigate the increase in real consumption caused by the fall in prices. But the net effect will be to reduce the resources available as real capital. This relative increase in unproductive consumption has important consequences in depressions, as we shall see in the next chapter.

4. We come next to the "positive" act—investment. It is fundamental to an understanding of the functions of capital, in health and in disease, that two points of view should be mastered. Firstly, it must always be interpreted dynamically, as a flow. Secondly, the habit of seeing it as a flow of goods in various stages, for various purposes, as well as a flow of money, must be acquired. We shall attempt to interpret the definitions rather in real terms as the money aspect is, perhaps, too familiar.

If we look at the productive machine at any moment, we see a vast organisation of plant and labour power working up a stream of goods through all their stages of growth. Since from the purely formal point of view capital is defined as against present consumption, we would at the outset class as capital all those goods not now available for consumption.[1] The word "now" is of course

---

[1] Stocks in the hands of dealers are not available for consumption in the strict sense, and are therefore capital.

necessary to allow for those goods which can only
be so consumed in the future, such as houses,
pleasure grounds, violins, and so on. Looking next
at the productive organisation we can proceed to a
further division. One section of the utilities there
embodied is in course of production: labour and
resources are being applied to it: ore is being mined,
seed is being planted, goods are being shaped, or
transported, or stored, against normal needs. This
is the flow of working capital from its first crude
form to its final pool in readiness to be fed into
consumption. It includes of course all the resources
which are being worked up into machines to aid
production.

The other section, known as fixed capital, has
already achieved its final form. It consists of
machinery, or cost-embodying organisation, which
have been created because it has been found that
they add to the productivity of economic endeavour. The cost they embody can be recovered,
if ever, only in the span of their working life.
Normally, a machine will decrease in value,
through time, as it slowly wears out, or as obsolescence increases the unit cost of its products
as against newer rivals. A broad distinction between these two types of capital may therefore be
helpful. Normally, we would say that, *ceteris
paribus*, goods which are working capital grow in
value through time; fixed capital-goods decrease
in value through time.

The firm grasp of working capital as a flow of

goods has been weakened in the development of
English economics by the insidious influence of the
Wages Fund theory. If we interpret working capital
as a stream of goods flowing up through their various specialised stages of production we shall see
that on its monetary side also working capital is
a flow—a revolving and also an elastic fund. For
the sale of goods at any stage in the process will
recoup the money fund for new investment at that
stage. The view that stocks of finished goods must
be in readiness to carry work-people over the period
of production is therefore a dangerous half, or
quarter, truth. Such a description has at most the
static verisimilitude of the lantern-slide as against
the fuller truth of the moving picture. We may
think of the process as a circular and never-ending
flow through a pipe. We can take any point as the
outlet into consumption. But here, also, there is no
break in the flow, since consumers pay producers,
normally, their costs; and these costs, so far as
they recoup working capital, simply return to the
continuous flow of working capital. The Wages
Fund theory embodies, in fact, an unfortunate paradox. For it leads to the view that working capital in
the form of money is inelastic. The truth is rather
that the supply of money will respond with considerable elasticity to a rising or falling demand for
real working capital. The money "fund" depends
on the credit system: and this, we have seen, is in
the short period relatively elastic under modern
banking conditions. It is rather the flow of in-

choate or unfinished *goods* which may be relatively inelastic in the short period. For once the real flow is interrupted, on the farms, or through an excess of stocks, considerable time and friction are inevitable before the flow of goods can be restored to normal again. Replenishment may need to start at zero, or even below zero, if plant has been forced out of commission.

These limitations will become clearer if we consider the idea of the period of production from the aspect of the elasticity of the flow at its various stages. We saw that the average length of the period of production for all goods would vary so far as resources were being pumped more, or less, rapidly into the first stages of the process.[1] This of course applies for any stage of the period. If expenditure is increased at any stage, if the application of materials and labour becomes more intense at any point of the process, then the average length of any one period of production will be increased or diminished according as greater intensity is applied nearer the inflow or the outflow of the period. With reference, therefore, to the elasticity of finished goods to "carry labour through a period of production," there will clearly be a definite lag. The outflow of final goods at the 1st of January 1934 depends quite definitely on the amount of investment at the beginning of the period that ended on that date, and on the intensity of work during that period: both factors

[1] P. 68 *et seq.*

having a definite limit of inelasticity. The same limitations also regulate the flow of goods at any stage of the period. The past escapes control and controls the future. For the future the outflow can to some extent be rapidly increased by more intense work on the stages just before the outflow. But this alone, if persisted in, would leave a void. The only final method of maintaining an increase in the outflow is to begin at the beginning and increase the inflow. Thus a stable increase in the outflow must lag behind the greater inflow by a period approaching a full period of production. When we consider the large proportion of raw materials that depend on agriculture, or extractive industry in its broadest aspect: and that a serious slump may force the abandonment of capital there —derelict fields and mines, damped down furnaces, diminished herds—we can well understand that this lag in the recovery of working capital may be even more extensive. It appears, then, that we here reveal the real inelasticity, as against an inadequate money flow, which may retard recovery.

It may be suggested that warehoused stocks may fill this gap. But this reserve cannot be adequate. Stocks are normally part of working capital. But "the tendency of every individual holder of the stock is to have no more than is needed to meet the usual demands from consumers, or from the producers who stand next in the order of transmission to consumers. Every dealer keeps enough in stock to meet current demands, and tries to keep no more. It is to his advantage to diminish his holdings to the minimum consistent with satisfying his customers. For every business manager, whether merchant or manufacturer, a needlessly large stock similarly means a needlessly large committal of his funds. . . . The drift in all must be to accommodate the supplies to habitual and expected demands, and to keep no excess."[1] Thus any additional holdings are speculative, or enforced by a fall in demand. In other words, they are *results* of the trade-cycle. Of course it is true that at some point in a falling price-level efforts will be made to liquidate stocks which have been caught by the turn. But this abundance occurs just at the wrong time, when demand is weak. The liquidation will add momentum to the fall in prices. This may help to maintain consumption, but this consumption will become more and more unproductive. For the falling prices will be steadily reducing the inflow, and the intensity in application, of working capital. So far as workers are being maintained out of the proceeds of taxation, and enterprisers are financing losses out of savings, consumption is being maintained out of *past* and at the expense of *future* work, not out of present production.

The point of view which, it is hoped, emerges from these arguments is just this. Working capital in the short period is the regulator of real income. It controls the flow of real goods from any given capital equipment. So far as applied to instruments,

[1] Taussig, *Wages and Capital*, p. 89.

it prepares an absolutely increased outflow of final goods for the future. The results of over-production in the capital industries are therefore intensified by the stoppage in the flow of working capital in these industries—with its repercussions on general demand. In the variations of working capital we see the magnitude of the variations in cyclical production.

H

CHAPTER VII

EFFECTS OF CHANGES IN THE RATIO OF
SAVING TO INVESTMENT

1. HAVING, it is hoped, clarified our definitions we shall begin to construct the theory by setting up a standard of reference. The most useful, because most definite, norm to take is that of an economic system in equilibrium. That is a system in which total money costs are equal to total incomes in such a way that on the average there is no incentive to increase or decrease investment; for there is no opportunity to make windfall profits (that is, profits resulting from prices being in excess of normal costs of production, including normal earnings of management). Also, there is no likelihood of windfall losses being made on the average. In other words, the price-level of final goods is stable, and is regarded as likely to remain stable; and in this condition of stability all the factors of production, including management, are earning their normal rewards on the average, no more and no less.

Next, we must bring into relation the two activities, Saving and Investment. If we begin with equilibrium conditions we can see that an increase in the total rate of saving, if all other factors remain the same, is bound to cause a decrease in demand; and that decrease in demand will itself destroy equilibrium. Similar but opposite reactions will follow from a decrease in the total rate of savings in the same conditions. Thus, while from the personal point of view saving is a neutral act, between hoarding and investing or spending, from the community's point of view it is a negative act: for an uncompensated change in the rate of saving has definite results. Similarly, starting from equilibrium, we see that an increase in the rate of investment, other things remaining the same, will increase spending and demand, and therefore upset equilibrium; and similarly for a decrease in new investment, other influences remaining unchanged. Thus the broad conclusion emerges that if there is an increase in the rate of saving, equilibrium can be maintained only if that increase in saving is exactly compensated for by an equal increase in investment—and *vice versa*. In sum, other things remaining equal, equilibrium is maintained only if $I = S$.[1]

One further conclusion strikes us from a mere consideration of equilibrium conditions. The rate of voluntary savings we should expect to remain fairly stable over the short period. It would of course grow absolutely as wealth increased, but it

[1] Meaning by I the amount invested during the period of time considered, and by S the new saving in the same period. Both I and S should be thought of in terms of money. I is then equal to the money invested, or, in Mr. Keynes's phrase, the cost of investment, within the given period. Then, if other conditions remain unchanged, where I continues greater than S, profits are bound through time to emerge, and a cumulative expansion of activity will follow—as is argued fully in the text.

would grow fairly steadily. For it depends on fairly stable practical, social and psychological conditions, such as the automatic savings of large incomes, the desire to secure a definite standard of living in the future, and the power to envisage that future. When we turn to the rate of new investment, however, we see that it is unlikely to maintain that correlation with the rate of new savings which is essential if equilibrium is to be maintained. For, whereas the rate of new saving is fairly stable, we should expect the rate of new investment to vary considerably in the short period. For tastes are constantly changing, new utilities and more efficient methods are constantly being developed: and in a system of private enterprise the probability of excess followed by glut is obvious. These facts demonstrate the probability that the rate of investment will exceed or fall below that of new saving.

So far, our conclusions have been merely deductive *a priori* probabilities. We must proceed to work out the results of such an excess or inadequacy in new investment. The rate of savings we take over from equilibrium conditions: it is the rate of savings of normal incomes, and it is likely to continue. If we, then, take a situation, which is likely to arise, in which new investment exceeds the equilibrium savings that have been invested,[1] we realise that a

---

[1] This is the most obvious cause of the development of disequilibrium during expansions. It can, of course, become effective, other conditions remaining the same, only if credit is expanded or the velocity of circulation increases. But other conditions may not remain the same. For instance, the rate of savings might

position has arisen in which windfall profits will
through time be secured by enterprisers. This windfall will constitute an incentive to further investment, and the new investment will reappear as
increased incomes in the pockets of those who help
in its production: incomes, or money demand will
increase.

If, then, the banks supply the necessary increase
in currency, this process will become cumulative.
The alternative situation that is likely to arise will
mean that enterprisers are suffering windfall losses.
The total selling value of their investment is less
than the money costs of production they incur, or
than the new savings that have been employed. A
decrease in investment will be entailed, involving a
limitation in total cost of production, and therefore
of incomes, and a falling off in demand. This again
will be cumulative, other conditions remaining the
same. In the first case I is greater than S, in the
second S is greater than I; and in both total costs
of production must diverge from the value of new
investment. Equilibrium must in both cases dis-
appear. The condition of the maintenance of equilibrium therefore is the maintenance of equality
between I and S. For any inequality involves dis-
proportionate changes in new investment. Of course

change rapidly because of an alteration in the incidence of taxation; or because of real changes in the prosperity of agriculture;
or because of a rise in efficiency earnings. In the latter case a new
rate of saving might arise as spontaneously as the new rate of
earnings. In these cases, if the monetary authority took no com-
pensating steps disequilibrium would follow.

there is no implication that equilibrium precludes development. I and S can both increase. But if equilibrium is to be maintained they must increase equally. Again, it is clear that rapid changes in the rate of saving will upset equilibrium. But this is unlikely to be an initiatory cause of the disturbance of equilibrium.

These propositions are of course fragmentary and preliminary. We must next attempt to outline the stages followed by the more normal type of trade cycle, as those who have developed this point of view have seen them. No trade cycle is normal. But understanding must begin with normality.

2. EXPANSION.—We shall start, then, from a position of equilibrium which is disturbed by some valid and important reason for an increase in the rate of investment. This point may be taken as the beginning of a new production period, so that resources will be fed into the intake of the period more rapidly, whether the ultimate outcome is to be fixed capital or a new type of final commodity. This new investment will also involve a more intense application of factors of production or working capital throughout its growth in the period of production. Taking these influences alone, then, we can deduce the following results. During the period of production the supply of final goods will not increase. But the money incomes of those supplying the factors of production *will* increase. Therefore there will be an increase in the price of

final goods: at least this is bound to happen if the rate of saving does not increase equally with the money demand caused by increased earnings. If it did, of course, the rise in demand due to greater earnings would be exactly cancelled by the fall in demand due to increased savings. But there is no reason to expect this compensation to take place. For savers have their reasons for saving, and investing enterprisers have their quite different motives for investing. In fact, we can assume that at the outset the rate of saving will not alter. It is worth noting also that we assume (in contrast to Dr. Hayek) that there are unemployed resources— an assumption that is realised, for the moment even under equilibrium conditions, when we remember the actual elasticity of credit and the reserves of stocks and labour.

This stage we can then define, following Mr. Keynes, as the primary phase. It consists in a rise in prices due to increased money demand for a static outflow of final goods. It will last according to the length of the period of production. For instance it will be longer, on the average, where the new investment takes the form of fixed investment; shorter if it is in consumption goods. In the latter case, and ignoring other influences, final goods prices will relapse to normal at the close of the production period. For the increase in demand will be met by increased consumption goods. Further, we must regard these influences, grouped under the primary phase, as continuously starting over again. For new production periods with new rates of input are beginning every day.[1] Thus the momentum of these primary phases is itself cumulative.

The relative increase in the demand for final goods which is characteristic of the primary phase has, however, fairly immediate repercussions which we can separate out analytically as initiating the secondary phase. For as soon as the prices of final goods rise above their equilibrium level, or as the turnover of final goods increases, costs not increasing proportionately, those who sell them gain a windfall profit, that is a surplus above the equilibrium earnings assumed before the new investment took place. Here appears the prime incentive to further investment—profits. All who sell final goods will increase their sales, and their orders for further stocks. And this upward jerk will extend down to the raw material. Thus increased investment will become general, if the banks take no steps to counteract it: and this movement will start as soon as the initial specialised investment begins to take effect in increased demand for an as yet unchanged output of final goods. Further, a general increase in profits will be the signal for demands for higher rewards by wage-earners. So long as there are extra profits to be made, concessions will

---

[1] This could not, however, apply, as rigorously as is indicated in the text, to those industries in which the possible production periods are determined by the seasons. But even there some elasticity is possible; for instance, resources can be transferred between different crops.

be accorded to these demands. Thus incomes will grow still more rapidly: demand will still further outstrip the flow of final goods, as yet bound to increase less rapidly than incomes, if windfall profits are being made. This argument can be applied to any period of time, for a new period of production begins each day. In other words, the process is cumulative day by day.

The dynamic forces of a situation in which I is greater than S can therefore be analytically separated on these lines. For firstly there is an increased demand for goods relative to goods available, due to the fact that an increase in the rate of output takes time. And secondly there is the emergence of windfall profits. If the banks acquiesce, both influences interact cumulatively.

3. TURNING PERIOD.—Why should these halcyon days end? We know that the central banks can "slit the thin spun life". But assuming that the abhorred shears are withheld, why should the process cease? For purposes of mere preliminary definition it is perhaps helpful to reply by a broad general statement, which simply cries aloud for further examination. We can then say that the upswing will falter when the increased outflow of consumption goods can no longer be sold at prices which recover their costs. But the reasons why this happens require very careful description.

First, then, we can say that the attractiveness of the prevailing new lines of investment will begin to fade as the fact that excessive production in them has taken place is realised. Combined with this is the effect of increased costs of production: the new ventures which later put to sea will be nearer the margin of safety—they will be fair-weather boats. When the new investment has taken the form of final goods, we should expect the recession to take place fairly rapidly, as their period of production is shorter. Historically this is illustrated by the restocking boom and slump of 1919–21. The fact, however, that one has to resort to such unusual conditions to find an example goes to prove that the normal case has been that in which the period of production involved has been longer. The centre of the disequilibrium is therefore to be found rather in the oscillations of investment in fixed capital. Nevertheless, though capital pro-duction be the centre of the typhoon, its ravages radiate through working capital, and will cul-minate in excessive production of final goods.

But this difficult analysis must be pushed even further. The word "excessive" brings us up against the crux of the problem: excessive relative to what? Our easy answer has suggested, excessive relative to the recovery of costs. But why cannot costs later be recovered? Our present theory offers an answer which has two aspects. It argues that output becomes excessive relative to the course of voluntary saving: or again that output becomes excessive relative to the amount of spending that is possible at the end of the investment peak. These two statements are of course the sides of one shield.

Let us recall the course of saving over the upward swing of the cycle. We saw that in any period of production during that up-swing the inflow of investment and its intensity of application will be increasing. Since the outflow is inadequate to the increased earnings that result, a rise in the pressure of total demand is inevitable, so long as the increased demand is not negatived by an equal increase in saving. But there is no reason to expect such an increase in saving. Total money savings at this level could be secured if those receiving higher earnings saved all the extra incomes they received: but to state this practical impossibility is enough. Thus the rise in expenditure is bound to take place. Having taken place, might it not be negatived by a factor we have so far ignored—saving forced by a rise in prices? This would imply that all those receiving fixed incomes (fixed for simplicity) would at once react by cutting their real expenditure to such an extent that their money savings retained not only the old proportion to their incomes, but an increased proportion sufficient to cancel the rise in prices. The growth in money demand through the increased earnings would need to be cancelled by equal money savings by fixed incomes: and these savings would be over and above the savings directed to maintain the old *money* proportion saved. For otherwise there remains a total increase on balance in money demand. Once again, a discipline so extreme is not to be expected, and does not in fact occur.

Therefore, starting from equilibrium, we can take it that, other factors not changing, there will be a rise in prices, where the rate of investment increases: and that this rise will be cumulative through the steady inflation of total incomes. But turn next to the outlet, the flow from which will be steadily growing, at first slowly, but on the completion of the first production period, suddenly and rapidly. While investment has been growing, we have seen that spending also will be increasing. In other words the extra costs of production have been spent by their earners before the goods which they helped to produce are ready for sale. So far as prices have risen the higher incomes have been dissipated in these higher prices. They will not have been applied so as to supply the working capital which will be necessary when the new plant has to be operated. Or to look at the matter in real terms, excessive expenditure will have prevented the flow of real working capital, or unfinished goods, from taking that form which they must take if the rate of investment is to be maintained. The growth in prices will further have helped to falsify expectations by raising costs. As the growing flow of final goods comes on the market, we should therefore anticipate a reaction in demand. For this flow will after a certain point expand more rapidly than the increase in incomes. Thereafter, so far as there has been excess production of any particular type of plant, the reaction will be immediate and severe. We can definitely say that such shocks are inevitable in the circumstances described.

This account of growing hesitation can be rendered more specific. We are justified in assuming that the normal *centre* of oscillation is the output of fixed capital. If, then, it is granted that there has been excessive spending on final goods in the upward swing, the growing output of *capital* goods must raise a new problem. For these new machines will require *increased* supplies of working capital, if they are to be operated. But they will at once be faced with the necessity to *raise* their money offers, or costs, in order to attract the working capital they require. The reason is, of course, not that the investment of total working capital has fallen—the opposite has, in fact, obtained; but that the increased spending on final goods that has taken place will have drawn the real resources available into those stages of production which supply finished goods for the spenders. Thus when the new plant enters into production it will find itself faced with two unfavourable circumstances. For, firstly, money costs will have risen as compared with the estimates made when the schemes were initiated. And secondly, resources will need to be "stolen", by the offer of higher rewards, from the final goods industries. Indeed, we may well expect an actual scarcity of real material working capital. For the expansion of the final stages for consumers will have taken the form of more intensive work near the outlet from the productive system. "Unformed" or "inchoate" raw materials will be relatively scarce. Here, then, we seem to put our finger on a real disequilibrium, in the form of inevitable shifts of real investment, which is bound to arise if the rate of new investment exceeds that of saving. In consequence, the expectations which launched the new investment in plant must be doubly disappointed.

Of course such falterings as these may avoid the fate of deterioration into a downward trend for trade in general: at least, for a time. The mainspring of new investment is still windfall profits, on balance. But many flimsy concerns will collapse at the first shock. Such bankruptcies involve immediate stoppages in the flow of working capital they previously supported. And the lean kine usually swallow some of the fat. The course of the crisis will thereafter depend on the reaction to such collapses. This reaction takes effect mainly through speculative and financial opinion: opinion which has been watching the course of expansion, and estimating the likelihood of its continuance. In the period of expanding profits through the sale of goods, we should expect that savings would be transformed into real commodities, including share holdings, rather than held in the form of money balances: for the former are appreciating, the latter depreciating assets. But once opinion begins to hesitate as to the continuance of such profits, the swing over may be intense. For much of the holding of shares and real stocks is quite unsound apart

from a continuance of the appreciation of their
money values. A hesitation in the rise of prices will
nip these specious blooms like autumn frost. Those
who have borrowed to hold shares, and who relied
on repaying their borrowings out of optimistic
profits will be faced with selling out at a loss. Those
who have correctly estimated the hesitation will
enter into their heritage. For they will sell forward,
and will use the money balances they have cherished
to buy the shares and raw materials they have con-
tracted to supply, when the date for settlement
arrives. Both influences tend to a rapid reversal in
prices; a bull market may be transformed to a
rampant bear with shattering and cumulative
rapidity: witness Wall Street in September 1929.
That we may not be dazzled with financial revolu-
tions only, it is well here to note that the tendency
to hold money, as it develops, will increasingly
withdraw money from its active uses as working
capital: and this just when an increase in working
capital is required by the new plant due for operation.

Of course, the banks may succeed in checking
the ebb by loans. But one of the factors on which
bull and bear speculators keep careful watch is just
the trend of banking policy. If, owing to the pressure of reserve proportions, there are signs of a
definite tightening in credit supplies, then the scene
is so far set for the revolution from bull to bear. In
these conditions, if banking policy has suddenly to
force market rates of interest above the equilibrium

rate, which will have been slackening with the hesitation in profits, then the reaction on speculative opinion will be immediate. The whole structure of analysis as to the effect of interest rates outlined in Chapters III. and IV. can, and should, in fact, be suitably worked into the saving-investment argument. For divergences between savings and investment, and between market and equilibrium rates of interest, are of course different aspects of the same organic economic situations. But, since the interest-rates aspect has already been analysed, it is not repeated here.

This account of the crisis has emphasised the diverse nature of the influences that operate. Each plays its part. Any one may seem to have taken control at different stages. In the United States excessive investment fostered excessive speculation; over-speculation drove home the initial hesitation of September to December 1929; banking policy later delivered the *coup de grâce*. But all these ingredients were necessary to the pudding. Those who have developed the saving-investment analysis have maintained an admirable catholicism. They have not claimed more than the position that the grasp of what is happening through changes in the savings-investment proportion is *one* essential step towards a solution. For it is the excess of the rate of new investment over the rate of saving that ultimately must generate a situation in which the outflow from the productive system cannot be profitably sold. So this type of analysis does not deny that monetary policy may prevent that position from emerging. It merely defines the position that will emerge if monetary policy does not prevent it.

4. SLUMP AND RECOVERY.—Next we must face the enigma of the slump. Why does it last so long, in spite of long-continued cheap-money conditions? We shall break in on the cycle where a hesitation in demand has deteriorated into a position in which windfall profits have turned into windfall losses, over the whole system. The weak have threatened the strong. As soon as insecurity is sufficiently widespread to cause new investment to fall below new savings, a different dynamic takes control. Apart from psychological exaggeration (to be examined later) this dynamic will emerge when the expectation of falling prices and windfall losses has become established. Thereafter, the slump of new investment below the rate of saving will realise and intensify this expectation.

This can be understood by two analytic stages similar to those used for the up-swing. Consider firstly a period of production at the outset of which a valid reason, such as a shock to investment expectations, has appeared for reducing the inflow rate of working capital. This implies falling total earnings to the factors of production, and therefore falling demand. At the same time the outflow of finished goods is increasing as the former increases in investment arrive at fruition. Here, then, we have circumstances compelling a fall in the price-level.

I

Secondly, this fall is intensified and consolidated if over the whole system the inflow of new investment (or the money demand it represents through earnings) falls below total money savings in the same period. For the only source from which a diminished demand through earnings could be compensated is an equal increase in spending through an inroad on the rate of voluntary saving. But the savers act from motives of their own. In a period of anxiety they will not become more extravagant. The reverse, in fact, is inevitable. And then a further fall in money demand is inevitable. So a more rapid fall in the price-level will be stimulated as the outflow of goods accumulates. Clearly this process can gather speed. Once the fall in prices has gathered way conditions are ripe for further inhibitions. Those new ventures which came rather late on the summer scene will at once suffer windfall losses. Their winter of discontent must be liquidation, or forced reorganisation. But as soon as total new investment falls below total savings net windfall losses will be a direct incentive to enterprisers to cut investment still further; and also to begin a direct attack on the levels of remuneration. The fall in total incomes will be accentuated by reductions in the rates of wages. And this secondary pruning will continue so long as windfall losses are being suffered. Unfortunately the pruning accentuates the tendency to windfall losses, and therefore to falling price-levels. The cycle is cumulative—a vicious circle indeed.

On this account of depressions, then, it is possible to distinguish two stages of the disease. If it is granted that the boom has developed conditions in which the outflow of finished goods cannot be profitably sold, then it follows that the remedy is the establishment of a scale of costs and a price-level for final goods at which the rate of new investment can be restored once more to equality with the rate of savings. Thus the minimum necessary liquidation of capital costs, of unprofitable concerns, and of efficiency earnings should be carried through as quickly as possible. If this is not done, the cart of the price-level will run away with the horse, the power unit, normal earnings. In ideal conditions this liquidation would be achieved as soon as the initial shrinkage in demand took effect through a decreased flow of investment meeting an increased outflow of goods. But we know too well that liquidation and falling earnings are dragged behind the decay of demand, for practical social reasons. In such circumstances the spring is bound to be pressed below its power of resilience. Losses become epidemic. Savings, instead of flowing into the reinvigorating channels of new investment, will be applied by enterprisers to maintain unprofitable output, or by the State to maintain idle labour. The slump has changed from an illness to a wasting disease. Revival must take the long road towards the development of new outlets for investment; and a slow and painful liquidation of costs, which might earlier have been cut short, becomes inevitable. The fire was lit by the initial shrinkage of demand. If that shrinkage is allowed to become cumulative through self-perpetuating losses, it will die only through burning itself out.

The enigma of the delay which in fact attends recovery from slumps can then be understood somewhat as follows. In booms, we saw, working capital is fed into the processes of production relatively too rapidly. In the later stages of the slump, the opposite disease will check recovery. For consider what has been happening during the depression. The channels of fixed capital have dried up rapidly. The flow of real working capital has dwindled in them; and this involves a diminution of the earnings of the agents of production, with its inevitable repercussions. The stream of unfinished materials evolving for consumers will have been barely maintained. But its real reproductive power will not develop adequately through the consumers so far as the latter are maintained in idleness. Looking at it from the money point of view, it appears that if over this diminished flow of investment losses are being made, then the flow will diminish still further. At the worst, the flow of working capital becomes orientated to the support of the flow of consumption goods, and largely disappears from the channels of fixed investment. Recovery must therefore suffer the delays and frictions of practical difficulties.

In this relative stability of consumption we surely discover the forlorn resistance to further

slump. This seems to be the real sticking point,
underlying the "solid core of gold" which Mr.
Hawtrey suggests as the limit of recession. For
everyone there is some lowest supportable standard
of living (barring collapse) in any actual social
conditions; at this point savings, where there is a
margin, will be invaded. But before the sticking
point is reached savings will be wasted, from
society's point of view, in providing goods at uneconomic prices to the community: corporations
will maintain some sort of dividends out of reserves,
and idle consumers will check the circulation of
working capital at the expense of losses by the
producers.

The remedy must be to make consumption once
more reproductive and more than reproductive. In
systems of private enterprise this can occur only
when all the agents of production are not earning
less than the total costs incurred. The hope of
improvement must at least be strong enough to be
acted on. At the worst, these will be the conditions
forcing the turn. The hard core of the standard of
living is threatened with invasion; savings will
begin to diminish. Obsolescence will have become
obvious; mere replacement will be clamant. More
hopefully, new possibilities for fruitful investment,
at least securing economic cost reductions, will have
established themselves.

Even so, recovery must be hesitant. For the real
working capital necessary to give it a flying start
will not be there ready-made. Stocks will be largely

liquidated, and recovery must begin with the raw material. The increase in investment must flow first into the narrow genesis of a new period of production. But if the dead wood has been cut away, and if monetary conditions are favourable, the stage is set for the up-swing. Here, then, we find the theoretical justification for the initiation of public investment by government. For as soon as windfall losses begin simply to reproduce themselves over the entire economic system, prices will continue to fall by the force of gravity—simply because they are falling. The disaster to avoid is that they should be checked simply by hitting the ground—the "hard core". The sooner this landslide is checked the less will be the sheer waste of depressions. At this stage it seems necessary to *create* reproductive consumption. This should secure that resources consumed will be earned by services which through their remuneration increase demand. The unproductive consumption which, for no extra effort, had battened on lower prices must be replaced by consumption based on additional production. If government can act discriminately, so as not to check necessary liquidation,[1] then public investment is one theoretical remedy for the chronic stage. In practice there seems little risk that the remedy will be applied too early or too widely. The

---

[1] "Necessary liquidation" is, in practice, a matter for an accountant, and even he will need to be omniscient to avoid some bad mistakes. In theory, all those concerns which cannot recover their costs under equilibrium conditions should be liquidated—and no others.

practical difficulties are all in the opposite direction.

5. In conclusion, we may estimate our progress by considering the advantages which the saving-investment approach realises.

Firstly, it is firmly based on what is in fact the actual dynamic of all human endeavour—the presence or absence of an effective incentive. This is in the true line of the British tradition. Since Adam Smith, the vital central position, in practice, of risk-bearing and the enterpriser has always been recognised. So, in this theory, the existence of residuary surpluses or deficits, after the equilibrium rate of earnings has been paid, is underlined as the incentive to or the negation of further investment; and this correct psychological interpretation of booms and depressions is worked out in definite terms of the real flow of productive activity. For it is shown that these windfall profits or losses are simply the balance between the total money value of new investment in any period and the earnings which remain unspent in that period: balances which clearly contain within themselves cumulative momentum.

Secondly, the influences of social psychology (which we shall examine later) can be readily fitted into this scheme. For the importance it places on incentive indicates the necessity for an examination of the motives to all economic activity, security and self-expression. It is not easy, in contrast, to combine psychological influences with purely mechanical explanations of cyclical fluctuations. But if we start by thinking in terms of future profits or losses, no such difficulty will arise. It is not of course therefore to be concluded that the saving-investment approach is suitable only to a system of private enterprise. The point here stressed is that this approach does start, as any theory should, with the motive to economic activity. If the motive changes, if for instance the State decides the proportion of new investment to saving, as it does to some extent, then the results of the system will alter. Motive and the bearing of risk will centre in the State. But the balance of State-controlled saving and investment will continue to determine the course of progress, though perhaps along different lines.

Thirdly, this point of view does help to illuminate the darkest corner of the problem—the long continuance of slump, and the slowness of recovery. Purely monetary theories are apt to seem unconvincing here. But this approach does think in terms of real movements in production. It shows up the inevitable delays of any necessary liquidation, delays which the facts verify. It indicates the cumulative tendency to windfall losses during this period; and by showing the reflection of these losses in unproductive consumption it reveals the real difficulties facing recovery. For it shows that the process of slump distorts the real flow of resources in relative favour of consumption industries; a distortion whose correction must be slow. Only

when savings, instead of being dissipated in unprofitable prices for final goods, can be profitably
applied again to employ labour in production can
real recovery begin. But this involves the emergence
of new prospects, new concrete schemes for investment. These depend on invention and opportunity,
as well as a revised list of costs. So delay is inevitable. Even when the new schemes are ripe for
commercial exploitation they will have to face delays due to the disorganisation of the raw material
supply-pipes.

Fourthly, it should be emphasised that the
saving-investment view makes no claim to be an
"open sesame". It is always conscious that it is just
one point of view. In Mr. Keynes's *Treatise on
Money*, for instance, this consciousness could not
be more obvious. The summary here attempted has
dealt with one point of view only, simply because
the monetary and rate of interest aspects have
already been discussed. But Mr. Keynes and Mr.
Robertson take pains to emphasise that these three
points of view (to which the psychological factor
can be added) are all complementary. They interact like the organs of the human body or the human
mind. Cause and effect is too limited a term of
explanation. Just as the condition of any one
organ is bound up with that of all the others, and
of the whole organism, so no complete explanation
of the trade cycle should be expected from any
one point of view. But the starting point should be
a point of view which radiates easily outwards to

include all the other aspects. This quality the saving-investment approach seems admirably to possess.

Finally, let it again be said that the reader should next repair to Mr. Keynes and Mr. Robertson. All here attempted is to afford familiarity with the main ideas necessary to the understanding of their works. Only the more normal type of cycle has been considered. But knowledge of the skeleton may aid appreciation of the living body. These two chapters are at best a preliminary canter. The jumps may now be easier.

CHAPTER VIII

UNDER-CONSUMPTION

1. MR. J. A. HOBSON's explanation deserves to be
thoroughly pondered, firstly, because it is the most
convincing statement of the inevitably popular
under-consumption type of theory, in British economic literature at least; secondly, because of its
admirable clarity; and thirdly, because it helps to
underline certain distinctions and definitions in
the theories just considered.

For Mr. Hobson, the cause continuously at the
root of the cycle is the unequal distribution of the
national income between the economic "classes".
By unequal is meant at once unjust and economically wasteful. From this unequal distribution he deduces a persistent tendency to over-saving; for income "which exceeds the customary or desired
expenditure of those whose felt wants are fully
satisfied"[1] is necessarily automatically saved, since
consuming standards are inherently conservative.
The next move is the proposition that hectic expansions followed by prolonged depressions must
result from such a "normal tendency to apply to
the production of capital goods a proportion of the

[1] *Economics of Unemployment* (2nd edition), p. 141.

aggregate productive power that exceeds the proportion needed, in accordance with existing arts of industry, to supply the consumptive-goods which are purchased and consumed".[1] "A normal tendency to try to save and apply to capital purposes an excessive proportion of the general income"[1] is a sufficient explanation of cycles: the normal excess of saving over spending is the final cause. For where the distribution of incomes involves the excess of saving over spending "it is certain that more production will be applied to producing larger increases of plant, raw material, and other capital goods than are capable of full and regular use in furnishing consumable goods to consumers".[1]

How, then, does the trade cycle actually develop under Hobsonian interpretation? Business men, when stocks after long depression are low, anticipate a recovery in demand. On this basis they place contracts with manufacturers for future deliveries; these contracts generating derived demand, and an increase in the credit basis. Especially, industries near the raw materials, mining, engineering, shipbuilding, are stimulated, because their increase is essential to an eventual increase in the outflow of final goods. So the creation of capital plant is intensified. The support of bank credit eager to unfreeze permits of rising prices, and therefore profits, as the new investment proceeds towards maturity; and producers make hay while the

[1] *Ibid.*

sun of rising prices shines. This account of expansion is familiar (if perhaps incomplete, especially as to the theory of working capital); and it needs no further elaboration.

The reaction arrives when it becomes apparent that the outflowing product cannot be remuneratively sold. Anxiety as to this may cause bankers and business men generally to draw in their horns, thus emphasising reaction. But the fundamental cause of the reversal (and here Mr. Hobson introduces his distinctive doctrine) is simply the fact that the increase in incomes resulting from the expansion is necessarily over-saved or under-consumed. This follows from the unequal distribution of the incomes, an inequality directly connected with the wage-lag during expansion. The cause of the turnover to slump therefore becomes obvious: for if over-saving is inevitable, the final goods resulting from the increased investment cannot secure remunerative prices when they reach the consumer's market. Without anticipating the review that follows, it is well to note the abrupt departure from the line of argument followed by the saving-investment theory at this point. For whereas Mr. Hobson's slump is generated in the expansion by under-consumption or over-saving of a permanent or absolute type, for the Cambridge economists *relative* over-spending in the *expansion*, or the excess of investment over saving, is the generator. This contrast is not quite so forcible as it here appears; for there is some difference as to the de-

finition of terms, especially as to spending. But it
remains the essential difference between the two
views, and will be later examined.

Once a fall in prices has started, the relation of
saving to spending is reversed. For whereas in expansion saving becomes excessive, when the reversal has gone some distance, "the proportion of
saving to spending is kept abnormally low". To
those who have accepted previous arguments this
may seem very mysterious. But perhaps if saving
be here interpreted as a synonym for the investment of Chapter VI. the riddle will be so far solved;
so far, for we must later analyse more deeply.
This "proportion" is not of course kept low through
any expansion in spending power; quite the reverse. The slump is, in fact, intensified by the effort
to liquidate excessive stocks in a limited market; yet
it must continue until these stocks are liquidated.

Perhaps what has been said may be taken as a
fair if unduly summarised description of Mr. Hobson's diagnosis. At its root lies the persistently unequal distribution of income. The steady result
must be over-saving or excessive capital production, leading to gluts and limitation of production
accompanied by under-saving and stagnation in
industrial progress. Throughout the whole process
there is continuous under-consumption, compared
to what would be rendered possible by a more
equal distribution of incomes. For such "equality"
would secure "a natural and right adjustment
between the proportions of spending and saving

in the aggregate income".[1] And this, in turn, would assure remunerative sales for the goods produced, as a result of the balanced rate of saving.[2]

2. What does Mr. Hobson mean by his two central terms, spending and saving? About spending he leaves no doubt. Spending is used as a synonym for final consumption. The theory is an under-spending or an under-consumption theory; and consumption is defined as the effective demand of final consumers for finished commodities. This then is clear. Spending is simply the correlative of saving in the sense we have previously accepted. So the amount spent and the amount saved together make up the total income. Of course, we did previously insist that savings were also spent so far as they were invested. But this was a further step in the argument. Mr. Hobson has a perfect right to his definition of spending as referring just to final goods.

When we turn to his definition of saving, however, we soon find ourselves in deep waters. In fact, in the writer's opinion, it is just the lack of definiteness and the ambiguity of Mr. Hobson's saving that prevent him from getting to the roots of the matter. Usually his saving appears as an equivalent for what the Cambridge School calls investment, rather than for their saving. Here is a typical example. "The real economic function of saving must be

---

[1] *Economics of Unemployment* (2nd Edition), p. 142.

[2] This summary is adequate for our purposes. But in justice to Mr. Hobson the student should go to his text.

kept clearly in mind. It does not consist in not spending, *i.e.* in putting money income in a bank, or even in making an investment. It consists in paying producers to make more non-consumable goods for use as capital instead of paying them to make more consumable goods, and consuming them." [1] Mr. Keynes would, of course, object that all capital is not destined to be used finally as fixed plant; and the objection would obviously be correct in the case, for instance, of many unfinished goods. But Mr. Hobson's saving is here on the investment side of the Cambridge fence, not on the saving side. The necessity to discriminate between them is either not recognised or not acknowledged. Yet almost at once he talks about "automatic saving and investment". [2] Now, while the negative act of saving can be automatic, it is difficult to see how this can be true of the positive act, investment. But Mr. Hobson often gives the impression that saving-and-investment might thus be joined by hyphens, as though some predetermined harmony saw to it that the one led to equal amounts of the other. Again, we are told that "falling interest does on the whole cause, or is accompanied by, a reduction in the rate of saving". [3] Certainly, on balance, it does have this effect on the voluntary saving we previously described. But it certainly cannot *cause* a decrease in investment as we have so far understood it. Here, then, it appears that Mr. Hobson's saving is on the *saving* side of the Cambridge fence. The fact seems

[1] *Op. cit.* p. 35.   [2] *Op. cit.* p. 36.   [3] *Op. cit.* p. 53.

to be that Mr. Hobson does not distinguish between saving and investment. So the risk is present that in this ambiguity he will slide into that meaning which suits the immediate difficulty. But in his more conclusive statements the two meanings are simply juxtaposed; as, for instance, "if there exists a normal tendency to try to save and apply to capital purposes an excessive proportion of the general income, we have a valid explanation of the actual phenomena of fluctuations and depressions".[1]

Now here we are clearly faced with issues of rigorous analysis, and of fact. Is it the case that saving and investment are different processes, and that they have different economic results: as all the theories we have examined assert? If they have not, then Mr. Hobson's diagnosis will be substantially justified. Yet, analytically, we must separate different influences. It seems evident that saving is in essence simply refraining from expenditure, and that as such its effect must be to depress industrial activity; whereas investment is just another type of expenditure which, as it issues in income, appears again as final demand. Further, as different motives direct saving and investment there is no inherent regulator which assures that the two processes shall proceed in harmony. We can of course conceive of an equilibrium rate of interest which would achieve this harmony. But in practice we have seen compelling reasons to expect divergence, not harmony,

---

[1] *Op. cit.* p. 141.

K

under the conditions of credit elasticity that obtain. In fact, then, the rate of interest tries to reconcile three streams, each to some extent an independent variable, saving, spending, and investment; and not just saving and spending. The equation of investment to refraining from spending on final goods precludes an examination of the really elusive difficulties—the effect of the period of production, of the different intensities in the applications of working capital, and of actual rates of interest. If we next refer to the facts our analysis is confirmed by the shrinkage of bank advances and, even more, of investment in depressions, whereas savings, though much diminished through losses, are hoarded in bank balances and in high-priced gilt-edged securities. If these be the facts, we must recognise them, and follow the analysis of the facts wherever it leads us.

The difficulties arising from this absence of distinction between savings and investment are illustrated by the following passage. Mr. Hobson is describing the over-trading of the expansion period, and he argues that the abundant credit "is primarily applied to stimulate the production of capital goods without any corresponding stimulation of consumption".[1] It is difficult to understand the absence of "corresponding" stimulation of consumption. For if we follow the course of events, it appears that investment in capital goods, following, let us say, equilibrium, is bound to increase consumption first.

[1] *Op. cit.* p. 78.

For incomes increase more rapidly than the outflow
of final goods over the bulk of the expansion period,
as we have seen. This appears to be merely an exact
description of the facts. In sum, during this period
there appears to be relative *over*-consumption—
that is, relative to the possibility of maintaining
equilibrium.

Mr. Hobson, of course, recognises this argument.
He agrees that "for a time free credit does put more
money into the workers' pockets. But it does not
proportionately raise consumption. For the rising
margin of profits on an expanding trade, taken in
conjunction with the wage-lag, means a larger share
of the expanding income for capital and a smaller
for labour. And this means, as we have recognised,
a larger proportion of saving to spending, of production to consumption, in a word, a quickening of the
process of over-production and depression."[1] But
in the statement "the new credit does not proportionately raise consumption" "proportionately" is
an insidious word. It may be that in expansions "a
larger share of the expanding income" goes to
"capital", "a smaller to labour". But the plain facts
which will affect the level of final prices and the
rate of profits are not this relative proportion, but
the changes in the demand for final goods relative
to the supply of these goods. If, through increasing
investment in the expansion sequence of production
periods, the demand for final goods increases faster
than the supply of these goods, then the seeds for

[1] *Op. cit.* p. 79.

further expansion are steadily sown. No matter what is happening to the relative shares in growing income, whether events favour capital or labour, if total demand for final goods outruns supply, then the effect of credit expansion has been to cause over- not under-consumption, relative to the possibility of maintaining equilibrium. (We remember, of course, that progress is consistent with equilibrium.) The only safeguard to equilibrium can be, *pace* Mr. Hobson, an increase in saving such as will cancel out the increased consumption by some of the earners during the expansion period.

A further issue may arise which should be faced squarely. Nowadays, when the bulk of consumption is done by wage-earners, references to over-consumption seem almost indecent. But, quite bluntly, the over-consumption referred to is entirely relative to the maintenance of equilibrium, or to the problem of the trade cycle. As here used, it has no social, no ethical connotations; for none such are discussed, although that argument could and should be developed. Few economists would fail to support the proposition that consumption is permanently inadequate as measured against any compelling ideal standard. All academic economists of any reputation share to the full the aspirations and bitter enthusiasms of Mr. Hobson. British economists from Adam Smith onward need yield to no organised body of men or thought in disinterestedness and toil for the general weal. But the first essential is to understand the trade cycle.

Thus most will share Mr. Hobson's eagerness for a more equitable division of the fruits of production. But most will admit also that this is essentially a long-period matter, as is also the development of the ability to consume.[1] For "now, as ever, the main body of movement depends on the deep silent strong stream of the tendencies of normal distribution and exchange".[2] It is doubtful whether men will ever regard any system of distribution as equitable; so that the equities promise us no release from the cycle. But when we turn to facts, can we deduce the short-period cycle from the mathematical fact of unequal distribution? It may well be that inequality does involve a permanent lowering of the supply of total economic welfare, a permanently limited market, as against what we all desiderate. But human nature also leaves something to be desired. And, as things are, the argument that inequality of distribution results in periodic over-saving, followed inevitably by glut, does not seem to the writer a correct description of events. For over-saving is a composite, self-contradictory term, as it is here used. It affords no standard even of theory, by which we can recognise a tendency to excessive activity. For when Mr. Hobson tells us of that "natural and right adjustment between the proportions of spending and saving in the aggregate income"[3] he offers us no

[1] Cf. *op. cit.* p. 34.
[2] Marshall, *Principles* (8th edition), p. 628.
[3] *Economics of Unemployment* (2nd edition), p. 142.

gauge by which to estimate the rate of progress that is possible. Only by splitting his saving into its two natural elements, saving and investment, can a firm basis for such a regulator be constructed.

Consequential points of divergence could be elaborated. But it seems wiser to concentrate on the main issue, the ambiguity lurking in the meaning of saving. Mr. Hobson's writings are so admirably clear that readers young in economic experience will profit most by repairing to his text, with the issue here discussed in their minds.

CHAPTER IX

PSYCHOLOGICAL

1. OUR survey would be incomplete without some consideration of the view that cyclical changes are caused by "the mutual generation of errors of optimism and pessimism". Here again Cambridge was a pioneer. Marshall, had he written on the Trade Cycle, would certainly have developed arguments very similar to those adduced by his disciple Lavington.[1] And the most modern statement of this view is to be found in Professor Pigou's *Industrial Fluctuations*. In this book it is not entirely clear whether psychology is regarded as a separate cause of rhythmic fluctuations: though Lavington gives pride of place to psychological influences. Certainly in an earlier essay Professor Pigou adduced psychological propagation as a cause of the trade cycle; that is, of *rhythmic* fluctuations. He also described it as an independent cause; for he argued that similar movements, though much reduced in amplitude, would follow from changes of mental tone even in a system of barter. *Industrial Fluctuations*, however, deals with fluctuations not

[1] See *Money Credit and Commerce*, where at p. 245 Marshall planned a final volume to deal with fluctuations—a plan never fulfilled. The extent to which he thought in terms of psychology is, however, evident in Book IV.

necessarily rhythmic: so there it can be logically argued that psychology may cause fluctuations, without causing *rhythmic* fluctuations. As will be later indicated, this position is much more convincing than any derivation of regular rhythm from psychological changes. But these rather fastidious points can be pressed too far.

Coming, then, to Professor Pigou's demonstration of the working of psychological causes: he tells us first that "these causes consist in variations in the tone of mind of persons whose action controls industry, emerging in errors of undue optimism or undue pessimism in their business forecasts".[1] "The various factors by which the scope of these errors is controlled"[2] are then explained. These factors are familiar, and I do not propose to amplify them. They are, firstly, inconstancy in the actual facts of industrial productivity and economic desire; secondly, the mental qualities of those who, through national or social custom, actually direct output; thirdly, the system by which funds are invested *via* joint-stock companies, including the partly anarchic system of company promotion; fourthly, the effect of business secrecy on the correctness of forecasts; fifthly, the control of output by a number of separate units, acting independently, either as competitors or as multiple monopolists, producing in anticipation of demand by roundabout methods, for markets which tend

---

[1] Pigou, *Industrial Fluctuations* (1st edition), p. 66.

[2] *Op. cit.* p. 67.

always to become larger and more speculative.
Most of these influences come under rubrics which
we have already considered.

This important doubt, however, arises. Would a
psychologist recognise these influences as in any
direct sense psychological? They are all surely
external characteristics of actual economic structure. Certainly they define the objective channels
through which the internal psychological forces
must flow. They set the limits within which instinctive forces and conscious motives have scope
to operate. They influence the subjective forces,
but they are not themselves subjective forces. And
it is with subjective forces that psychology deals.
It is therefore suggested that some examination of
the subjective forces which do operate, the reasons
for their operation, and the methods and results
of their operation, is called for.

Professor Pigou does proceed to explain the
factors which actually promote the generation of
errors. Firstly, he points to "a certain measure of
psychological interdependence"[1] among business
men. "There comes into play a quasi-hypnotic
system of mutual suggestion."[2] Here an internal
force is put forward; but little more is said of it;
and it certainly requires amplification from the
psychological point of view—as to how suggestion
operates, and as to what is suggested. The sequel
will attempt some initial steps in this direction.
Then, secondly, it is pointed out that an error in

[1] *Op. cit.* p. 79.   [2] *Ibid.*

forecast by group A does influence the demands of other groups. And, thirdly, the pervasive debtor-creditor relationship does tend to spread any such errors. To these last two factors the remarks previously made apply. They are, of course, immensely important. But they are facts of external structure, not internal or subjective forces dominating economic activity from within. The psychological forces behind the sequence of events have not been described, although, in the very long period, the external factors mentioned may result as a sediment from these forces.

It may here be noted that the psychological explanation has an obvious attraction in that it does help to explain why we should all be depressed, or optimistic, together at the same time. For we are all equipped with the same instincts; and these instincts operate in the same way in each one of us; whereas no such unanimity in result is true of conscious thought;[1] so that one would not expect that the same intellectual errors would be made together by all those who control economic activity. This suggests that we must delve deeper to the actual instincts which control our "tones of mind" if we are to explain this unanimity at all convincingly. Sir William Beveridge has criticised Professor Pigou's argument on this very point.[2] So far as "error" means intellectual error, the affirmation

---

[1] Or of information consciously absorbed, on which judgments are made. Cf. p. 160.

[2] *Unemployment*, p. 333 note.

of universal error is false psychology. But if we examine the unconscious internal forces behind forecasts and investment, there the justification for this universality may be found.

Professor Pigou then completes his description of the cycle by pointing out that "errors of either sort . . . have the characteristic of generating, after a while, errors of the opposite sort".[1] The reasons for this reversal are examined. Especially, every period of gestation has its conclusion. "For all things, there is some period of gestation, the conclusion of which brings forecast to the test of fact. When this test has been applied to a fair number of things and found wanting for a fair number, confidence is shaken."[2] Sir William Beveridge has remarked on the difficulty which arises from the fact that different industries have different lengths of periods of gestation;[3] but the discussion of this point is not relevant here. Further, Professor Pigou points to the way in which bankruptcies "detonate" through the debtor-creditor relationships, especially if banking policy is unwise. To these two arguments the comments previously made apply. These are objective structural channels, not subjective forces.

Professor Pigou does, however, adduce one truly psychological explanation of this reversal at crises. "An industrial boom has necessarily been a period of strong emotional excitement, and an excited

---

[1] *Industrial Fluctuations*, p. 83.
[2] *Op. cit.* p. 84.   [3] *Unemployment*, p. 333.

man passes from one form of excitement to another
more readily than he passes to quiescence."[1] And
again: "business failures necessarily and always
breed fear among industrialists that their own
debtors may fail".[2] In each of these quotations an
internal force of an a-rational[3] kind is indicated.
During panics at crises we do see this swing-over;
and a change-over from optimism to panicky
pessimism may be a broadly true description,
though a fairly protracted period of anxiety inter-
venes. Also, during depressions, the influence of
fear, checking enterprise, is clearly present. Perhaps
it is unduly restrictive to limit the activity of fear
to the nexus of the debtor-creditor relationship. Its
influence, for instance, on the immensely ramified
"economy campaigns" in depressions is obvious.

These psychological hints, however, need analysis
and amplification (for the quotations given above
are exhaustive). We should certainly define more
exactly what types of forces are operative. What is
optimism or pessimism? What is fear? Are they
emotional, or intellectual, or instinctive forces?
What type of force can set the snowball of suggestion a-rolling, or does it need any force? The answers
will explain the type of result we should expect
from their activity: in fact, such an analysis alone
can explain these results psychologically, as to

[1] *Industrial Fluctuations*, p. 85.
[2] *Op. cit.* p. 87.
[3] Just as a-moral conduct is conduct outwith the moral world,
and therefore not influenced by moral ideals, so an a-rational force
is one not influenced by logical reasoning.

whether they will be invariable in the same circumstances, or as to how alterations of the circumstances
may modify them.

Psychology has, in fact, much to tell us here. The
task of applying accepted psychological sequences
to economic facts is certainly one which should
be approached with extreme caution. But without
such an application there can be no psychological
theory. An examination along these lines will
therefore be attempted.

2. We can begin by considering the adequacy of
the word "error" in the phrase "errors of optimism
and pessimism". It has been cogently remarked
that the bulk of individuals do not in fact err from
their own point of view, in their reactions to the
cycle.[1] If general prices are rising, it is no error to
secure profits while these are easily made. Lord
Morley refers to a remark of Queen Caroline about
the Triple Alliance of 1735 which illustrates, though
it somewhat exaggerates, the individual's frame of
mind here. "It always put her in mind, she said, of
the South Sea scheme; people went into it knowing
that it was all a cheat, still hoping to get something
out of it; everybody meaning when he had made his
own fortune to be the first in scrambling away, and
each thinking himself sharp enough to be able to
leave his fellow-adventurers in the lurch."[2]

It is, of course, no answer to the logic of this

---

[1] *E.g.* by Hawtrey, *Trade and Credit*, p. 99
[2] Morley, *Walpole*, p. 203.

attitude to say that these are only money profits. For while conditions remain as at present, the individual is better with money profits than without them. And once they are made there are ways of conserving them which can be utilised by individuals during slumps. Similarly, it is no answer to say that the individual should realise that, if equilibrium were maintained, society would be better off. For the individual must also recognise that, from his point of view, social and economic organisation has to be taken as given; he alone cannot alter it. Thus, except for those caught by the swing-over from rising to falling prices, there is no individual error. It is therefore indicated that we should substitute for errors a less definite term; say, excesses of optimism and pessimism.

On the other hand, if we say that the error is made by society, we encounter further difficulties. For society can hardly be said to err; unless indeed it is assumed that there is a "social mind", an idea sufficiently metaphysical to be here ignored. Certainly only a reasoning consciousness can err. What does happen is that there is social waste as a result of these individual excesses of optimism and pessimism. In fact these individual activities are excessive only relative to the avoidance of social waste. That such social waste does result from the cycle will hardly be disputed. For instance, it is the cycle which necessitates a large part of the reserve army of labour.[1] Thus, even if at present the cycle is an

[1] *Is Unemployment Inevitable?* p. 95.

inevitable result of economic progress, the ideal remains to secure the progress without the cycle, through more adequate methods. Once again, excess seems the more suitable term.

In sum, then, error seems too intellectual a word to be properly linked with optimism and pessimism. For errors are seen, and immediately cast out, by different minds at different times. Minds abhor errors, once they recognise them, just as nature abhors a vacuum. It is, however, not only possible but in every case actual that individuals can combine conflicting *instincts*. To go no further, it is at the root of the human problem that the instinct of self-assertion or aggression conflicts with that of social feeling.[1] Yet both co-exist all the time in each one of us: not, of course, consciously in specific cases—for then we would take steps to resolve the recognised conflict by rational means—but certainly unconsciously.

So we shall consider the view that excesses of optimism and pessimism give rise to the social waste which results from the trade cycle. We shall do this in the confident hope that our text will be accepted by psychologists as a justifiable psychological hypothesis at least. For a purely rational explanation like generated error they would not consider within their sphere. It is, of course, common knowledge that we tend to manufacture rational explanations for conduct which springs largely from our unconscious urges. Every poli-

[1] Cf. Freud, *Civilisation and its Discontents*, pp. 99, 102.

tician, every elector, exemplifies this.[1] But if our explanation is to be psychological it must unravel these unconscious sources.

3. The phrase "mutual generation" of these excesses next requires examination. This is the process which causes the generalisation of optimism and pessimism. As Professor Pigou says, suggestion can be the only contagious agency. (His "quasi-hypnotic" adjective may be ignored here for reasons that will appear later.) Now suggestion is a recognised psychological process; and some enquiry into what psychologists mean by it should be helpful.

We may start with McDougall's well-known definition: "Suggestion is a process of communication resulting in the acceptance with conviction of the communicated proposition in the absence of logically adequate grounds for its acceptance".[2] The term suggestion is often broadly used to describe the whole process; but it is also applied more specifically to emphasise the cognitive aspect of a process which has also its emotional and conative sides.[3] From the emotional side the process operates through sympathy, from its conative side through imitation. Biologically, the value of the mechanism has been that through it a suitable reaction to a stimulus is obtained in each member of a herd with the utmost rapidity. Thus when danger is

[1] Cf. Hart, *Psychopathology*, p. 103.

[2] *Social Psychology*, p. 83.

[3] "Conative" can be taken roughly to mean unconsciously purposive.

sensed by one member, a whole herd will at once take to flight although no direct contact with the source of danger has been established in the great bulk of its members. According to Rivers, the term suggestion should be applied only to unconscious influence: for conscious influence is really a quite different process, especially as it permits of variations from the original pattern under the criticism of conscious logic.[1] He gives as an example of unconscious influence the exercise of social tact: and anyone who has suffered the disappointments of trying to be consciously tactful will warmly agree.[2] Of course, it is obvious that the weapon of suggestion can be consciously *used*, for instance, to aid recruitment during a war. But even so, the reasons why it is used may spring largely from the unconscious; and only if its influence is accepted unconsciously, is suggestion actually operative.

When we explore their texts further, however, we are brought rather to a halt by the fairly unanimous assertion of the psychologists that in itself suggestion explains nothing. Ginsberg, for instance, after referring to an opinion of Hart in the same sense, affirms that "to refer any form of behaviour to suggestion in general is not in any sense to give an explanation of that form of behaviour".[3] The reason for this unanimity is recognition of the fact that suggestion in itself has no motive force, but

---

[1] W. H. R. Rivers, *Instinct and the Unconscious*, p. 91 *et seq.*
[2] *Op. cit.* p. 97.
[3] *Psychology of Society*, p. 30.

L

is merely a mechanism through which any particular force is conveyed to others. It secures that action will be identical in different members of a group or community; but it does not define what that action will be; and from the incentive to that action its dynamic must be derived. Suggestion is the microphone: we must find the speaking voice.

When we ask what these fundamental incentives are, the psychologists give us a definite answer. They are the instincts. Thus it is the instinct of each herd member to flee from danger that supplies the force behind the stampede. Without this incentive suggestion could effect nothing. But, based on it, suggestion is the process through which the force is released and generalised for the safety of the herd. It may, then, be wise to complete this introduction by stating briefly the main characteristics of an instinct. Instincts are "innate dispositions", that is, invariable tendencies, to respond to stimuli in a definite regular manner, quite independently of previous experience or conscious thought. This regularity of response should set us thinking about the fact of regularity in the "mental tones" of different phases of the trade cycle. It appears that suggestion alone cannot explain why there is such regularity of tone; but that if we dig deeper to the instincts behind the mental tones, psychology may lead us to firmer ground.

We must, in fact, refer the phrase "excesses of optimism and pessimism" to our psychologists, and ask them if these can supply the forces which are essential before suggestion can spread them. Their answer will not perhaps be quite unanimous. But the dominant reply will be that optimism and pessimism are not original sources of action; they are rather emotions derived from the successful or unsuccessful activity of instinctive forces. Mr. Shand, indeed, describes desire as "a very complex *emotional*[1] system which includes actually or potentially the six prospective emotions of hope, anxiety, disappointment, despondency, confidence and despair".[2] But he also states that "it is a complete mistake to represent desire as an independent force".[3] If, then, we resort to actual experience we can, I think, see that the instinct to act is fundamental, and separable from the emotion, *e.g.* in a panic. Any combatant who has been badly wounded in face of the enemy will testify to the fact that he at once experienced an overwhelming impulse to get away from further danger. So devastating was this almost physical pull that his consciousness was otherwise nearly completely bare. The rabbit was jerked to his burrow. This surely goes to prove that the force behind unconscious action is an innate disposition to react to certain situations in a definite regular way; in fact, an instinct.

If these arguments are sound, instinctive action takes this form. A certain set of facts, or a stimulus, will let loose an instinctive force, which will be coloured by a definite emotional tone, depending

---

[1] Italics mine.   [2] *The Foundation of Character*, p. 463.
[3] *Op. cit.* p. 519.

largely on the extent to which the instinct is satisfied. If the real cause is then removed, the unconscious tendency will lapse. A suspicious noise at
night may cause you to scream or run; but if you
realise that a picture has fallen the instinctive
response disappears. It may be thought that these
examples are too crude. But the unconscious is
crude. Indeed, it is at its crudest that the instincts
are revealed most plainly.

Coming back, then, to the suggested dynamics,
optimism and pessimism, on the line of argument
we have offered the following comments arise. We
should agree that these emotions would spread
through mutual generation in certain circumstances. But we should consider it more important,
psychologically, to define the instinctive forces of
which they are the emotional colourings. Of course,
it is not denied that extreme stresses of emotion can
for a time freeze the springs of action. But this is
the abnormal not the normal situation, and we shall
refer to it when we deal with panic. Secondly, we
should require to ascertain the nature of the real
situation whose persistence is the basis of excessive
optimism and pessimism accompanying the suggested instinctive activities.

The next step, therefore, is to define the instincts
which supply the dynamic in response to a continuing stimulus.

4. Whence, then, comes the force which overflows
in excesses of optimism or pessimism? It is wise

here to go back to first principles. If we do so, we
shall find that the predominant human instinctive
forces are grouped under two major forces: firstly,
social feeling, or the gregarious instinct; and,
secondly, the individual's striving for significance,
with its intellectualised gradations of security and
power. I have put this contrast in its broadest
terms, as, for instance, Adler does.[1] For our purpose
a broad statement is most useful. We do better to
keep to the agreed highway, however intriguing
some by-paths may appear. This fundamental
diarchy of the instincts will in fact be found expressed in different forms by all psychologists.
Freud,[2] for instance, groups them under Eros and
aggression, and insists no less strongly than does
Adler on the importance of their conflict as the
root of the human problem. Of course, for men and
women the problem is complicated, almost re-
created, by the fact that self-conscious rational processes are also operative. Individual reasoning
power, in fact, maintains and emphasises the
diarchy by, so far, tending to underline the individual's interest; whereas in the case of bees and
ants for instance, the social instinct is practically
supreme. Yet in most herds we find examples of
co-existing instincts which at times emerge in open
conflict, as in all mating contests. Of course the
biological justification is here obvious; but the same

[1] Cf. *Understanding Human Nature—passim.*
[2] Cf. *Civilization and its Discontents*, p. 102. Cf. also Rivers,
op. cit. pp. 52-53.

could be argued of conflicts in human societies. When we consider the importance of group organisation, the unity within groups and also the particularism of groups in relation to the integrated community, then the co-existence of these two conflicting parent stems of instinctive force stands revealed. The importance of the problems raised by their inevitable clashes need not be laboured.

It is also unnecessary to dilate on the reason for the overflowing of the self-regarding instincts into *economic* channels in modern times. There is no doubt at all that wealth is one of the main avenues to the expression of the individual's significance. Perhaps the ultimate reality of this is somewhat flimsy. But in relation to accepted standards, money is certainly a magic key.

It might be thought that the obvious instinct to light on as the basis of economic particularism is the acquisitive instinct. I have not chosen this course, firstly, because there is some doubt as to whether such an instinct exists.[1] The urge to acquire may be implanted through what Graham Wallas calls the social heritage—or tradition. It is at best an offshoot of the instinct of self-preservation. Then, secondly, it seems more important in such a general introduction as this to concentrate on fundamentals and to secure as broad a basis as possible. The course chosen certainly does this. The evidence for an instinct to construct is also fairly convincing,

[1] Cf. Rivers, *op. cit.* pp. 53, 266; *Psychology and Politics*, p. 36; McDougall, *op. cit.* p. 277.

and equally relevant to economic activities. But it also "can be regarded as primarily a manifestation of self-preservation".[1] Thus, apart from incidental references, we may ignore these two streams.

There is one apparent difficulty which can be usefully considered at this point. We have fixed on the self-regarding instincts as the dominant individual incentives to economic action. But the mechanism of suggestion is generally explained as organically related to the gregarious instinct. Its usefulness consists in securing the safety and cohesion of the herd. It might then be asked, can suggestion be properly combined with individualistic instincts, such as self-preservation? For, allied to these, it might positively encroach on the wellbeing of the community. In answer, it must be emphasised that original simple mechanisms in animal life cannot be rigidly applied to human societies, except as initial analogies. Suggestion, as it operates in society, is in fact a graded process adapted in the course of human development to new circumstances. This is especially obvious in the activities of social groups within the State. These groups illustrate an ascending scale of organisation, from the mere crowd based on physical contact to those with carefully constructed channels of action and communication, such as the British Medical Association. As Hart says, "the distinction

[1] Rivers, *Instinct and the Unconscious*, p. 53. An obvious example is nest-building in birds. Children also prefer making brick houses (or mud pies) to many elaborate toys. Similarly, there is real economic incentive in the creation of an efficient business.

between individual thought and crowd thought is not a fundamental difference of kind, but merely one of degree".[1] Similarly, we could construct a scale of groups in order of suggestibility ranging from a Paris mob to a committee of intellectually disinterested metaphysicians.

In fact, the mere presence of common action is sufficient to give scope to the influence of suggestion. But most groups also embody an element of rivalry. Rivalry is also one essential element in group activity. The institution of private enterprise is itself just another example of co-existing social feeling and rivalry in group formations. It is at present part of our economic tradition. Though it may so far conflict with social well-being it also certainly subserves the purposes of the wider group to a definite extent.

We need therefore have no scruples about combining the effects of suggestion with the economic incentive. For where we have rivalry there also we have some element of social feeling. Of course, if particularist activity clearly endangers the safety of the community, the reaction *via* the social instinct will be strong. But "endanger" is normally too strong a word.

5. Let us, then, return to suggestion and consider how it operates to over-emphasise the individual instinct for security or significance in an a-rational way. We agree that so far as the instinct steadily achieves satisfaction it will be coloured by con-

[1] *Psychopathology*, p. 116.

fidence; so far as it is baulked it will generate
anxiety or despondency. Also so far as it is rationally grounded it will develop into a rational motive:
but at present we are interested in excesses.

Now the reason why excess is apt to be generated
through suggestion arises simply from the fact
that suggestion is invariably accompanied by the
inhibition of rational criticism. Here psychologists
speak with confidence in a way that should interest economists. They tell us that the incentive
to the suggested action is protected from the im-
pact of conflicting critical ideas by the very nature
of the process through which it is passed on between
individuals. As well as emphasising the dynamic
to act in the suggested way, suggestion cuts out
the influence of the thought processes which would
indicate the risks of that course of action. A man
acting under the influence of suggestion is like the
commander of a submarine observing his enemy
through a periscope. He sees his easy prey and is
impelled towards it: but his periscope cloaks from
him the surrounding dangers. The extent to which
suggested springs of action can escape rational
criticism will be realised by anyone who recollects
the type of conduct towards the enemy that was
dominantly approved by the public, and was in
fact to some extent adopted officially during the
Great War.[1] Then of course the instinct towards
self-preservation was in flood; rational criticism
was blocked, was in fact considered unpatriotic.

[1] Compare the Preface to *Heartbreak House*, by G. B. Shaw.

In the economic cycle, then, we should expect that conditions which are in fact favourable to the making of profits would act as an incentive to the instinct to positive self-realisation. We should also expect that this instinctive force would be spread by suggestion; whence it would follow that the dynamic would be over-emphasised because it would not be controlled by rational criticism. This seems to be a sufficiently exact summary of the psychology of the cycle's upward swing, put in psychological terms, that is, explained from the point of view of subjective activity. Only from such an aspect can explanation claim to be psychological; and its adequacy must depend on the correspondence of this subjective sequence to the actual facts.

How far, then, is this outline true of the dynamics of economic motives? Considering enterprise first, it appears that the business man reacts to two types of influence; he thinks of prospects in his own firm and industry, and of the general tone in industry as a whole. As to the first he is, on the average, in the best position to judge, and his judgment is in control. As to the second he is certainly more suggestible. Here he is in a position fairly similar to that of the average investor. Yet surely it is exaggeration to say that in conditions other than those of crisis or acute depression, either the enterpriser's or the investor's judgment is inhibited. Can we truly say that psychological excess dominates their judgment, especially when we re-

member that most of the time they are right from
their own point of view.[1] Is it not truer to say that
their judgments are in control?

I should prefer to put the matter thus. The instinct to express one's own significance can be
taken as constantly operative, whether it debouches
in the form of increased investment or an intensive
pursuit of safety. Where, then, actual conditions
favour investment, we should expect achieved
success in that direction to be confidently toned,
and *vice versa*. We should further expect some accentuation of the positive or negative instinctive
force through suggestion, but not to such an extent
as *in itself* to dethrone judgment, or alone to cause
a reversal from positive to negative. In other words,
while psychological forces will help to emphasise
real disequilibrium, it is still the real industrial and
economic conditions which determine the course
of the trade cycle; psychological causes can at most
accentuate its amplitudes.

This point of view is driven home if we face the
following question: On psychological grounds only
is there any reason why the industrial tone should
be optimistic, or pessimistic, for *regular* periods of
fairly similar length in successive cycles? Can psychology explain why hope or despair lasts for two or
three or four years regularly? In sum psychology
cannot explain rhythm; and rhythm is the crux of
the cyclical problem. Of course it is not denied that
psychological forces may take control during crises.

[1] Cf. p. 147 *ante*.

But this will be considered in the next section, where, following our previous practice, we shall try to summarise the psychological course of a cycle.

6. We need not labour the expansion, as the general argument has been indicated. An actual situation, in which, through investment conditions and banking support, profits are to be made, will set the self-regarding instincts positively to work to secure them. Suggestion will help to spread the incentive and will impose its periscope to shut out rational doubt. In these circumstances, suggestion will not emanate from one authoritative source, and in this lies its distinction from that acme of suggestion, hypnotism. Hypnotism is, in general, an artificial, submissive relationship of patient to leader, and most of its force it owes to that leader's prestige. In non-Fascist countries and where free enterprise retains considerable scope, hypnotism can hardly influence economic motives.

Suggestion will disseminate the urge to make profits rather as one type of rumour grows. Dr. Hart, in a very stimulating article, says: "A rumour does not always arise as the result of a succession of reports proceeding from a single centre of origin, but sometimes seems to show a kind of spontaneous evolution, growing similarly from many distinct centres."[1] The effectiveness of this type of suggestion can be realised when we consider how we feel impelled to pass on and slightly embellish any

[1] *Op. cit.* p. 111 *et seq.*

rumour or story, at every opportunity. The amazing
rumour of the Russian troops passing through
Britain in 1914 to the western front (which was
quite unfounded in fact) illustrates both these
characteristics. It also indicates the wish-fulfilment
nature of many rumours, a source especially relevant to economic psychology.

In normal circumstances, we have argued, these
unconscious influences will do little more than
exaggerate an actual tendency. But towards the
peak of the cycle psychological forces may often
take control. This is especially probable when the
threat to the garnered power of self-expression
becomes great. A general scramble of the *sauve qui
peut* type is to be expected on such markets as the
Stock Exchange, especially as there the emotional
ties cementing the group instinct are very tenuous
indeed.[1] The revulsion from bull to bear sentiment
is certainly exaggerated by psychological forces,
though an interval period of *anxiety* should be
noted. In fact, after the hectic stage a type of
collapse occurs in the speculative markets which is
quite in line with individual psychology. Where the
instinct to self-preservation is frustrated, "collapse
with tremor seems to be especially characteristic of
Man".[2] But though the crisis panic is of this nature,
it is yet just the burst into flames of a fire that has
long been smouldering. It is a result, not a cause.

[1] Cf. Freud, *Group Psychology and the Analysis of the Ego*, p. 46
et seq.

[2] Rivers, *Instinct and the Unconscious*, p. 56, where examples are
given.

During the slump, the instinct to self-expression will of course continue to operate. But it will take the negative emotional tone of exaggerated pessimism. Fear for individual security will accompany timidity in investors and spenders; and this will be spread by suggestion, some of which may be of the prestige type emanating from the example of government. The result will be that action will be canalised towards securing safety by a timid and to some extent self-contradictory policy of cutting expenditure.

Thus both in expansions and depressions the correct balance between the social instinct and self-expression is upset; in the one case, by excessive acquisitiveness, in the other by excessive solicitude for self-preservation. Of course disaster may accentuate social feeling. This clearly has been President Roosevelt's firm foundation since he assumed control. And this accentuation is to some extent present in all depressions, when efforts to mitigate the lot of those who suffer most are always developed.[1] Still, the swings in psychological economic motive appear to me to occur in the successive forms taken by the self-regarding instinct.

As to the revulsion from excessive pessimism to growing optimism, I am unable to suggest any explanation on purely psychological grounds. Certainly our normal frame of mind is constructive; and when the causes of paralysing fear are removed

[1] Compare the excellently directed prestige suggestion of the Prince of Wales in relation to unemployment.

the desire to create will assume its natural control.
But this does not take us far.

7. We can now summarise the more important
results which emerge from this discussion.

Firstly, it appears that psychology cannot explain
rhythm or regularity in the temporal ups and downs
of the cycle, and in their amplitudes. Professor
Pigou himself reverts to real or structural causes to
explain the lengths of the recurring swings. "The
interval between the two sorts of error", he says,
"is partly dependent on the time that it takes
business ventures to yield their fruit and partly
upon the intervention of specially good or bad
harvests or other external accidents."[1] So we shall
have to repair to saving and investment and monetary influences to explain rhythm.

This psychological approach does, however, teach
us something about the internal side of the dynamics
behind private enterprise. It does explain how
exaggeration takes place; though it insists that
suggestion and emotion are not in themselves
dynamics. It confirms the view that such exaggeration must be based on the presence of real conditions in contemporary economic events, which in
turn must stimulate innate instinctive dispositions.
Suggestion cannot operate without something to
suggest. It cannot alone explain a depression lasting
three years. Thus we are driven down to the deep
roots of economic motive. Of course the roots do

[1] *Is Unemployment Inevitable?* p. 102.

not explain the flower. But if suggestion is offered as an explanation, then to the roots we must go.

So in a sense we seem to have learned little. The gist of the argument seems to be that psychology does not in itself offer any *direct* explanation; except to the extent that the conflict of the fundamental instincts to self-expression and to social cohesion is an explanation. And this seems so very deep-seated that it does not much enlighten us. Directly, it tells us little. For it is rather a truism to say that the trade cycle is just a result of the failure to maintain a correct balance between the development of self-expression and the welfare of the community. In this sense the roots of the cycle penetrate right to the fundamental problem of human societies. The gradual solution of this problem marks the stages of progress; and therefore the cycle may just be one of its necessary concomitants. Of course the cycle *as we know it* is bound up with the system of private enterprise. A solution at this stage would not abolish the clash of individual and social purposes. Yet it is at least interesting and salutary to realise, if our argument is sound, that the cycle is so deeply founded. Reliance on superficial remedies will at least be discounted. And the type of annoyance often expressed about the discouraging tendency of economists to suggest that these fluctuations are inevitable, will be turned aside when it is realised that the problem is just one aspect of the eternal social problem.

Then again, what has been attempted is the mere alphabet of the subject. For simplicity we have

talked of the individual. But economic results are
shaped nowadays by groups with individualist
aims partly at one, to some extent at odds with the
welfare of the community. A psychological analysis
should therefore examine the motives and influences
of such groups as organised markets, trade unions,
professional associations, the press, the banks,
government departments, and so on. But this so far
is uncharted ocean.

Finally, it should be noted that psychology has
its own cure for a disastrous clash of instinctive
forces. This is a practical method employed by
psycho-pathologists; but it also opens new vistas to
all kinds of social endeavour. It is of course the
process of sublimation; a process by which, to quote
Rivers, "the energy arising out of conflict is diverted
from some channel which leads in an a-social or
anti-social direction, and turned into one leading to
an end connected with the higher ideals of society".[1]
The relevance to the type of instinctive disturbances involved in economic activities is fairly clear.
Owing to the imperfect integration between individual aims and social welfare, individual instinctive forces are over-stimulated, then blocked. Only
if the blocked energy is guided into the wider
channel of social progress can it at once achieve its
satisfaction, and excesses either of optimism or fear
be avoided.[2] This seems a long period cure indeed.

[1] *Op. cit.* p. 156.
[2] Interesting comments on the prospects of the sublimation of
economic nationalism will be found in Allyn Young, *Economic
Problems* (*Economics and War*). The rationalising of instinctive

M

Still, those who have, for instance, experience of regimental life will realise the transformations of the self-regarding instincts that sublimation can achieve. Of course sublimation can be rationally organised—in fact, this is the ideal. For so far as a person's knowledge is not organised, so far he remains suggestible. But rational sublimation will fail so far as it does not understand the roots of the trouble. The rational policy in economic life would then appear to be to strengthen all those influences which express the social instinct, always under an adequate conception of social welfare. By this course the mere frustration of the self-regarding instincts will be avoided. Once again this process seems endless. Yet, even so, I cannot refrain from one further quotation on this point from Rivers, most acute, most sympathetic, most lamented of our younger psychologists. Speaking of the disequilibrium produced by war, he says, "I believe that we may look to this instability as the source of energy from which we may expect great accomplishments in art and science".[1] This is relevant to the thought that the swings of the cycle may be negative aspects of positive progress, as Mr. Robertson argues.[2]

I should like in closing this chapter to disclaim

forces has, however, its own peculiar excesses. Refreshingly sane observations on the risks it runs will be found in *Plan or No Plan*, by Barbara Wootton, at p. 330, where the economic motive is discussed.

[1] *Instinct and the Unconscious*, p. 158.

[2] Cf. *Banking Policy and the Price Level*, pp. 19-23, for a splendidly balanced discussion of this issue.

any suspicion of dogmatism. The approach ex-
plored is perhaps novel, and is certainly halting
and inadequate. It has been offered largely in the
hope that it may incite those who are better
equipped to correct its errors and develop any
validity it may have.

CHAPTER X

SYNTHESIS

1. SUMMARIES are dangerous. This is especially so
when the subject is as involved and many-sided
as the trade cycle. A mere synopsis cannot do
justice to the scope and intricacy of the argument.
But if this is granted and constantly borne in
mind, there may be some advantage in a final rapid
review of the line of our progress. It is important
to make explicit what has indeed lain implicit in
the order and growth of the analysis: the fact that
all these theories can be cumulatively combined,
and must be so combined, to attain a reasonable
solution of the problem. The object of this summary
is to suggest the shape of such a synthetic theory—
that and nothing more.

Turn back, then, to our initial definition of the
problem. An examination of the facts established
the existence of sufficient regularity in the expansions and contractions of industrial activity to
justify the hypothesis that some recurrent and self-
generating cause or causes are at work. It then becomes the task of theory to construct a logical
justification of this hypothesis in relation to these
facts. How far has success been attained?

On the monetary side it was argued that the self-

generation of expansion, turning-period, and recession had been satisfactorily established. For with
prevailing systems of elastic credit in which the
final control of the central bank is bound to be
applied too late, conditions in which profits are
created and the process grows cumulatively, are
bound to emerge. In such circumstances, the time
must come when central banks will enforce the
cessation of credit expansion; and then some recession is easily accounted for. But it was further
argued that this type of interpretation did not
suffice to explain the length and intensity of the
depression periods. For depressions last longer
than the advent of cheap money conditions and
abundant potential credit. It was therefore necessary to undertake an examination of the effects of
the expansion period on the structure and flows of
investment.

Firstly, it appeared that the power of our banks
to expand credit carried with it a factor which at
once affects the balance of production. For if credit
is so expanded the actual rate of interest will be
kept below the equilibrium rate. This result is inevitable in the existing structure of the banking
system. It follows that an expansion of future
goods will be stimulated greater than would be
possible under conditions of continuing equilibrium.
Another aspect of this situation is the fact that
where credit is expanded in this way, the rate of
new investment will exceed that of saving. And
on this line of analysis, an attempt was made to

define as exactly as possible the meaning of excessive investment.

At the outset it was affirmed that the investment in plant was excessive in the sense that the possibility of its recovering its costs when it came into production was prejudiced from the outset. The reasons for this failure to recover costs were, however, more difficult to elucidate. The first suggestion offered was that during an expansion period in which I is greater than S, just because investment feeds on credit expansion, the rate of voluntary saving is insufficient to support the new investment. This, in turn, means that during the upswing spending is *relatively* excessive; it is excessive relative to the maintenance of equilibrium. This means that as expansion proceeds, demand concentrates more and more on final goods. Thus when the successive productive periods begin to reach their conclusions and the new plant is ready to produce *its* quota of final goods, it is met with a system working to near capacity, with all the slack of real working capital already attracted into the production of final goods. The new plant will therefore need to bid higher for its necessary share of working capital, and to suffer the frictions of inadequate mobility. It will also be faced with higher money costs for labour which has won a share of the expansion in profits. The further fact that the output of final goods must increase with the added flow from the new plant, whereas the flow of money demand will diminish as investment slackens when these conditions are revealed, will set the stage for reaction.

Reaction may follow from the above circumstances alone. This will be more likely when the period of gestation has been long, and the possibility of over-investment and relative over-spending is therefore the greater. But the check to credit expansion may itself be the immediate cause, and will, in any case, be likely to intensify the investment-saving reaction.

Thereafter the trail of the slump is marked by the fall in prices. Under the burden of costs that lag behind this fall, losses and dwindling investment are inevitable. Working capital shrinks in the channels of capital investment, spreading its repercussions in a further shrinkage of demand. If liquidation could anticipate slump, and if investment could then be re-stimulated, depression would be temporary. But in actual circumstances, liquidation is dragged behind the fall in demand. The very rigidity of the increasingly intricate *technical* stages of production intensifies this lag. For it adds to the lack of mobility in the transfer of productive resources. The inhibitions of human anxiety supply the human motive to that defensive attitude which is so apt to tighten the shackles of depression. Where all are defending their own ground, a united attack on the enemy is difficult to organise. At the worst the descent can end only by hitting the ground, when savings must be encroached on, when depreciating capital must be renewed, and when more efficient methods of production have been discovered.

In sum, there seems to be an inherent error in the timing of the processes of competitive production. The expansion of investment in capital plant crowds into a fairly short period in response to the time during which the demand for final goods is increasing most rapidly; and this occurs considerably before the peak of the cycle. This is the natural response of private enterprise. But that very concentration involves wrong timing at the end of the period of gestation. The effects of this flaw in the timing are worked out through the actions and reactions of saving and investment.

Lastly, the importance of private enterprise and the dynamic of profits, which had emerged in the previous analysis, indicated the necessity of examining the psychology of the motives behind this type of economic system. Some consideration of pure psychology taught us that it is insufficient to remain satisfied with mere emotions like optimism and pessimism as the sources of oscillations in economic activity. The incentives behind them could be only instinctive. And the alternating forms taken by the self-regarding instinct were broadly indicated as the instinctive sources. These alternate forms were defined as, firstly, the urge to the expression of personal significance, with its perhaps acquired systems of construction and acquisition; and, secondly, timidity in face of a threat to one's security. On this basis suggestion finds grounds for

exaggeration which are psychologically valid. The
conclusions which followed from this analysis were,
however, so fundamental that they could not throw
much light on the practical mechanism and immediate causation of the cycles. Suggestion, in fact,
requires a continuing real cause if it is itself to be
continuously operative. Such a real cause can be
found only in the conditions which create the alternating periods of profitable and unprofitable enterprise revealed by the monetary and investment
theories.[1]

Considering these theories together, then, it
appears that they do make out a theoretical case
for the existence of rhythm. The psychology of the
actual economic dynamic does supply the broad
conditions in which over- and under-activity would
alternate. In monetary and investment institutions
we further discover structural reasons why expansion should be followed by recession, why such
recession should decline into stagnation, and why
stagnation should be cured only by a slow painful
reorganisation which prepares the soil for the
emergence of new possibilities. The monetary elasticity of credit reacts on investment possibilities,
and *vice versa*; and both operate within the channels
laid down by the forces which inspire private enterprise. That being so, only a system of explanations

---

[1] This summary has been included to indicate the mere thread
of the argument. It is well, therefore, to repeat that to follow threads
is to do injustice to the pattern. All the fully grown theories of the
trade cycle are living, developing systems of thought. To summarise
them is to kill them.

can do justice to the systematic disease we have to understand.

So fluctuations about the output trend are to be expected. The further problem remains: can reasons be given for the comparative regularity in these fluctuations which the statistics suggest? A word may be added on this—perhaps the most difficult conundrum among the many raised. How can the actual duration of the cycles be explained? And why do different cycles last for relatively similar periods?

2. We can begin by remembering the expansion which takes place during a period of production in which new investment is fed into the system more rapidly than new savings become available. At the end of such a period the possibility of a check arises, because the new output, probably excessive under competitive conditions, will exert a moderating influence on price-levels. As the production period of consumption goods is comparatively short, we might expect this check to arrive perhaps one and a half to two years after the increased investment in plant was initiated. It has been estimated by Mr. Kirk that both the expansion and the liquidation periods in agriculture will vary within similar limits.[1] Thus in those countries in which agriculture predominates, a short cycle of some three and a half years is to be expected. The United States provides the classic example here. The

[1] *Op. cit.* p. 213.

short cycle is not, however, strongly marked in the
relatively more industrialised European countries.
   In the latter communities it is to be expected
that the check caused by the increase of final goods
at the end of an expanding production period will
for a time be more readily overcome by the repercussions from increased investment in capital goods.
This investment will steadily reappear as increased
demand in the hands of income and profit earners,
if the banking system does not apply the brake.
The influences of investment in fixed capital bring
us therefore to consider the longer, and, for European countries at least, the major cycle. Now, there
is an obvious limit by which such investment is
bound—the optimum producing capacity of the
system. After that point, costs will inevitably rise.
Further expansion will be damped down. This will
mean that the rate of increase in the demand for
final goods will tend to become steady, instead of
expanding. A rapid fall in the demand for plant
will then follow. Professor Pigou has noted that
there is no dynamic rhythmic force in this negative
optimum load limit.[1] And certainly the reasons for
subsequent recession have to be revealed.
   The line of explanation which has appeared most
convincing is that the over-investment in plant
brings with it maladjustment in the different flows
of investment. Its distribution has favoured goods
for the too distant future relative to those for
the present. When, therefore, the maladjustment is

[1] *Industrial Fluctuations*, p. 207.

revealed, the cessation of activity in the constructional industries will be drastic. This maladjustment results inevitably from the expansion of credit, for credit creation involves the reduction of the actual below the equilibrium rate of interest. It is a subsidy to future goods, relative to present goods. So far, therefore, as the creation of credit is cumulative, the maladjustment of the supply of future as against present goods is also cumulative. It is in this latter *real* form that the malign aspects of credit elasticity become operative. This cannot be rapidly adjusted. For all the frictions connected with inadequate mobility of the agents of production at once come into play. Unemployment of these agents breeds cumulative depression; and timid saving may intensify the grip of stagnation.

As to the length of this longer cycle, the first explanation that suggests itself is to connect it with the average life of capital plant. It might be thought that such an average represents so scattered a dispersion that its value is limited. Strong reasons have, however, been given for accepting a pronounced mode of ten years.[1] If this be accepted, the sequence would be somewhat as follows. The jerk upwards would take the form of a rapid expansion in plant based on the arrival of new prospects. Once this jerk is granted, the cycle would follow the lines previously indicated. The negative check would

[1] Cf. Pigou, *Industrial Fluctuations*, p. 208. A fuller account will be found in *A Study of Industrial Fluctuations*, by D. H. Robertson, p. 36 *et seq.*

appear some fairly short time after the optimum load of the system had been reached. But as the *expansion* in plant had been concentrated within a short period, so in ten years' time the need for its *rehabilitation* would be also concentrated. It would appear as a further potential jerk, if other conditions were not unfavourable.

Further, however, it seems to the writer that the durations of the up-swings and the down-swings must be given separate examination. For they respond to different conditions. For instance, taking expansions first, the level of development reached will be one such condition. As the more obvious physical needs become satisfied, demand will become more changeable. The margin of error in estimates will increase.[1] Again, the rate of invention varies considerably as between different long periods. Since this carries with it the rate of obsolescence, one would expect the expansion periods to differ in length as between these different long periods. So far as we can divide the course of economic growth into stages,[2] we would expect relative similarity in the lengths of expansion periods in any one such stage.

As to the duration of slumps, silence might be the wisest course. In the past, no positive comprehensive steps have been taken to cure them. For the provision of cheap credit can hardly be called more than negative. It is certainly true that when cheap

---

[1] This point is admirably elaborated by Mr. A. Loveday in *Britain and World Trade*, pp. 86-94.

[2] Cf. p. 17 *ante*.

credit implies also a reduction of the actual below the equilibrium rate of interest the incentive to investment is more than negative. But if over-expansion of capital goods has gone far in the previous expansion this situation must be slow to arrive. For the equilibrium rate is bound to approach zero until the real disequilibrium is liquidated. In these circumstances the period of stagnation is almost inevitable. And it brings with it nowa-days so many troubles of an international political type especially, about which scientific prediction is impossible, that the expectation of any exact similarity in duration would be quite unwarranted. Under the past type of treatment, however, it seems reasonable to presume that stagnation might well continue until the need for improvement in the capital equipment became obvious. But here again the emergence of inventions might expedite recovery.

These remarks are fragmentary. They may, at best, be suggestive on a matter which has so far not been thoroughly analysed.

3. Finally, what remedies are suggested by our analysis? And to what extent can each effect a cure?

At the outset, a sharp distinction must be drawn between mere palliatives and more radical treat-ment. In fact, the adequacy of palliatives should be more directly questioned than has been the case in the past, in view of modern developments. It has often been argued that cutting off the high and

low peaks will be sufficient. Certainly, half a loaf
should not be scorned. But the recent dead weight
of unemployment must throw doubt on its final
adequacy. Quite bluntly, if the British economic
system has to carry an average of a million unemployed because of the trade cycle (and this would
seem a roughly fair estimate in relation to post-
war facts), then it would appear that radical treat-
ment will be necessary. The future will probably
more than cancel the effect of palliatives. For the
long-period tendency will almost certainly be
towards ever wider markets: and until some
measure of solution is found for the problem of
the frontiers (economic as well as political) this
will entail still heavier unemployment in depressions.[1] It seems, in fact, that the necessity to
grapple with unemployment is taking the place of
waste in production as the centre of the cycle
problem. If that is so, the radical remedy will be
ever more steadily to limit or at least to supple-
ment the scope of private enterprise. It has always
been recognised that full employment could be
given—at a price. But while the increase in wealth
was regarded as the central aim, and while private
enterprise was accepted as the means of attaining
it, no direct cure for unemployment could be
planned. If the emphasis is changing, the reduction

---

[1] Cf. J. M. Clark, *Strategic Factors in Business Cycles*, p. 119,
where the view is expressed that, other influences remaining unchanged, the intensity of the cycles will tend to increase in the
future, because of "our rising standard of living and especially the
increasing importance of durable consumers' goods".

of unemployment will be sought even at the risk
of a less rapid increase in wealth. The difficulty is
that men refuse to accept one of providence's firm-
est decrees—the impossibility of eating a cake and
having it. The tariff issue need hardly be cited in
proof of this obtuseness.

With this broad introduction we can proceed.
From the purely monetary side, it does not seem
possible to expect much more than some reduction
of the swings. Certainly, a fuller realisation by
central banks of the influence of credit creation on
the movement of actual relative to equilibrium
rates of interest may be expected to result in some
diminution of the rate of expansion, and also of
the duration of slumps. The time is therefore ripe
for the freeing of the Bank of England from some
of its statutory obligations. We noted that elasticity of credit at a price diverging from the
equilibrium level is inherent in our present system
of joint-stock banks; and that the check to that
elasticity is bound to come too late. Some tightening of the Bank of England's control is therefore
overdue. This thesis has been so thoroughly developed in the Macmillan Report[1] that the point
need not be elaborated. The abolition of the old
restrictions on note issue, and the freeing of the gold
reserve for purposes of international stabilisation,
are involved. But even when the Bank has the
power rapidly to adjust credit, can we expect that
it will have the knowledge and technique necessary

[1] Committee on Finance and Industry, Cmd. 3897.

to wipe out the cycle? Perhaps it could do so for a
closed British system. But the difficulties of international financial co-operation it cannot now control. Further, this is no mere question of stabilising
prices, as we have seen. Rapidity of circulation
has also to be leashed. Where the expansion of real
capital is based on credit expansion in a system of
private enterprise, the possibility of *radical* or
complete cure through banking control seems to
the present writer unreal.[1] The cycle is inherent in
private enterprise. Of course, a radical cure may
bring with it even greater ills—"that we know not
of". In fact, so far as the amplitudes of the cycles
can be reduced, thus far does the argument that
the price of private enterprise may be worth paying
gather force.[2] For the price is the waste of the
cycles. Here the future must decide, though recent
experience has weakened this argument. In the
meanwhile, any estimate of the extent to which the
amplitudes of the cycles may be reduced by wiser
control belongs to the realms of prophecy, not of
science.

This increase in the flow of money demand
through a spurt in investment brings us to the
second group of remedies. Here again there are

---

[1] Cf. J. M. Clark, *op. cit.*, p. 208. It is interesting to find so
distinguished an American economist thoroughly sceptical about
the possibility of radical cure through credit control, in view of
contemporary knowledge and technique. But, when we remember
events in the United States since 1929, it is not surprising.

[2] Cf. D. H. Robertson, *Banking Policy and the Price Level*,
pp. 19-23.

obvious palliatives. Investment excesses, such as occurred in 1928 and 1929, have always inspired their belated cures. For instance, the proposals of the Macmillan Commission would limit the ravages of some company promoters in the healthiest way possible; by putting a permanent institution in their place. The Stock Exchange has also taken action to avoid the diseases that then ran riot. Particulars of sub-underwriting agreements must now be lodged and approved, before permission to deal will be granted; and generally the conditions have been tightened so as to prevent the unloading on the public of shares in immature or merely speculative companies. But there is no need to elaborate these remedies. For while they are useful and necessary, they come after the event. They deal rather with the orgies of the feverish expansion stage. They do not cut to the roots of the disease. It is to be feared that while these roots remain, the ingenuity of future gamblers will be very equal to forcing speculative blossoms in the hot-house air of an investment boom.[1]

When, however, we seek a radical cure on the lines of the savings-investment theory, we are brought face to face with the fundamental issue. So long as the initiative in investment is left in private hands, disequilibrium between the rates of new investment and saving appears inevitable.

[1] Remedial action through Government stimulation of investment has already been considered at pp. 42, 85, and 124. It is not therefore further referred to here.

For conditions in which windfall profits can be made are certain to arise; and these circumstances carry with them relatively excessive investment in plant. The cyclical logic then completes its course. We may learn to diminish the length of slumps by a more rapid liquidation of uneconomic costs and enterprises. But the heavy weight of ignorance and timidity precludes a rapid recovery under present circumstances.

So we are finally thrown back on what is the ultimate issue—the psychological diarchy. This in turn, of course, takes political shape in two practical policies. Our last task must be to define this issue. The conclusion that emerges from the argument is that so far as private enterprise remains in control cyclical movements will also continue. Mitigation is possible. It may prove sufficient. But caution suggests that palliatives can do no more than painfully restrain the vagaries of the future. The only radical cure for the excesses of the self-regarding instinct is the direction of its energies into activities satisfying social requirements also. The issue lies, in fact, between private enterprise and social organisation; between what is usually regarded as the most efficient wealth producer, and a system willing to sacrifice some of this assumed surplus in the endeavour to secure fuller employment.

Like all social issues, this one runs the gravest danger of being drawn much too sharply. Professor J. M. Clark has admirably expressed the sane attitude to the problem of the future relation between

private enterprise and social action "There is", he
says, "a mutual interest which should be strong
enough to produce fairly adequate action, if industry can be organised in such a way as to make this
interest effective. Whether this degree of organisation can be brought about without going so far as
to make the system of private enterprise impossible
is a question which can be answered only by the
process of experiment."[1] Opposites can be combined
—they certainly must be in actual life. There should
be no need to emphasise the material benefits which
private enterprise has conferred on society. It also
satisfies and supports some fundamental virtues
in human nature — self-reliance, energy, courage.
Control which squanders these values is a disaster.
Sublimation is quickly said. But the dangers of "sublimation" enforced from above should be evident to
anyone who considers the wastage of the attempt to
socialise agricultural production in the U.S.S.R. Sublimation cannot be imposed; it must be discovered,
and enthusiastically ensued. Yet the excrescences of
private enterprise can be cut away only by direct
attack, direct organisation, from above. In this connection it seems probable that the campaign against
unemployment will develop from its present negative stage into a positive long-period organisation
for the provision of useful work. From the communal point of view unemployment is unused
capacity. From that angle, the cost of maintaining
labour is a social oncost. It continues whether the

[1] *Op. cit.*, p. 197.

labour is employed or not. And idleness has irreparable human costs, which add to the social deficit, though figures are impotent to measure them. To prevent this idle capacity from being spilled, and becoming positive social waste, a nationally approved organisation always engaged in creating useful work for those thrown idle in the competitive system has been shown by harsh modern facts to be essential. On some such lines a way of reconciliation may be found, granted the will to construct it.

But this is to raise a further issue.

APPENDIX 1

UNEMPLOYMENT PERCENTAGES

(1860–1921—Trade Union Figures
1922–1933—Official Figures)

1860 .	1·85	1885 .	8·55	1910 .	5·1
1861 .	3·7	1886 .	9·55	1911 .	3·05
1862 .	6·05	1887 .	7·15	1912 .	3·15
1863 .	4·7	1888 .	4·15	1913 .	2·1
1864 .	1·95	1889 .	2·05	1914 .	3·25
1865 .	1·8	1890 .	2·1	1915 .	1·0
1866 .	2·65	1891 .	3·4	1916 .	0·45
1867 .	6·3	1892 .	6·2	1917 .	0·6
1868 .	6·75	1893 .	7·7	1918 .	0·7
1869 .	5·95	1894 .	7·2	1919 .	2·5
1870 .	3·75	1895 .	6·0	1920 .	2·55
1871 .	1·65	1896 .	3·35	1921 .	15·55
1872 .	0·95	1897 .	3·45	1922 .	14·3
1873 .	1·15	1898 .	2·95	1923 .	11·7
1874 .	1·6	1899 .	2·05	1924 .	10·3
1875 .	2·2	1900 .	2·45	1925 .	11·3
1876 .	3·4	1901 .	3·35	1926 .	12·5
1877 .	4·6	1902 .	4·2	1927 .	9·8
1878 .	6·25	1903 .	5·0	1928 .	10·9
1879 .	10·7	1904 .	6·4	1929 .	10·6
1880 .	5·25	1905 .	6·25	1930 .	16·2
1881 .	3·55	1906 .	3·7	1931 .	21·7
1882 .	2·35	1907 .	3·95	1932 .	22·1
1883 .	2·6	1908 .	8·65	1933 .	20·0
1884 .	7·15	1909 .	8·7		

APPENDIX 2

Indices of Wholesale Prices

	Board of Trade. Prices of 1900 = 100	United States (Aldrich Report and Bureau of Labour). Recalculated to basis 1900 = 100	Germany (Herr Schmitz). Recalculated to basis 1900 = 100
1871	136·0	$136\frac{1}{2}$	117
1872	145·8	141	130
1873	152·7	$135\frac{1}{2}$	135
1874	148·1	$132\frac{1}{2}$	124
1875	141·4	126	116
1876	138·0	116	113
1877	141·6	116	$113\frac{1}{2}$
1878	132·6	111	104
1879	126·6	107	$94\frac{1}{2}$
1880	129·6	$118\frac{1}{2}$	$105\frac{1}{2}$
1881	127·3	$117\frac{1}{2}$	103
1882	128·4	$120\frac{1}{2}$	100
1883	126·8	118	98
1884	114·7	110	$93\frac{1}{2}$
1885	107·7	103	$86\frac{1}{2}$
1886	101·6	102	82
1887	99·6	103	$84\frac{1}{2}$
1888	102·7	$104\frac{1}{2}$	90
1889	104·0	$104\frac{1}{2}$	$94\frac{1}{2}$
1890	104·0	103	101
1891	107·4	102	$98\frac{1}{2}$
1892	101·8	$96\frac{1}{2}$	89
1893	100·0	96	86
1894	94·2	87	$77\frac{1}{2}$

	Board of Trade. Prices of 1900 = 100	United States (Aldrich Report and Bureau of Labour). Recalculated to basis 1900 = 100	Germany (Herr Schmitz). Recalculated to basis 1900 = 100
1895	91·0	85	77
1896	88·2	82	77½
1897	90·1	81½	79½
1898	93·2	85	84½
1899	92·3	92½	92
1900	100·0	100	100
1901	96·9	99	94
1902	96·5	103	93
1903	99·9	103½	94
1904	98·3	103	94
1905	97·6	105	97
1906	100·5	111	106
1907	105·7	118	113
1908	102·8	111½	106½
1909	104·1	115	105
1910	108·8	99b	..
1911	109·4	95b	..
1912	114·9	101b	..
1913	116·5	100	..
1914	117·2	100b	..
1915	143·9	101b	..
1916	186·5	124b	..
1917	243·0	176b	..
1918	267·4	196b	..
1919	296·3	214b	..

(b) 1913 = 100

INDEX OF POST-WAR PRICES

	Board of Trade 1913 = 100
1920	307·3
1921	197·2
1922	158·8
1923	158·9
1924	166·2
1925	159·1
1926	148·1
1927	141·6
1928	140·3
1929	136·5
1930	119·5
1931	104·2
1932	101·6

The indices for 1871–1919 are taken from Layton, *Introduction to the Study of Prices*, p. 151.

APPENDIX 3

NOTE ON FORCED SAVINGS

IT is evident that for Dr. Hayek the villain of the piece is an undue expansion of credit. This is clearly revealed by his animadversions on the effects of forced savings. He criticises those who look to forced savings as saviours of the inadequate flow of voluntary savings in times of expansion: that is, inadequate relative to the inflated demand— not, of course, to the "optimum demand". Against this view he states quite bluntly, "it is probably more proper to regard forced saving as the cause of economic crises than to expect it to restore a balanced structure of production".[1] He notes that "forced saving takes place whenever the volume of money is increased, and does not need to manifest itself in changes in the value of money". This is, of course, true.[2] When prices do not change the forced saving that takes place is certainly of a rather more negative type than when they rise. For as the value of money is steady, the effect on those whose incomes do not expand is that they are prevented from sharing in the increase in output due to more efficient productive methods. It still remains true that the production of future goods is over-expanded for a time. The only possibility of preventing the development of this disequilibrium in these circumstances lies in a *reduction* in prices. For this reduction would increase the demand for present goods relatively to that for future goods, the latter demand being damped down by the failure of money profits to increase. The obstacles to this remedy under existing financial conditions are very obvious.

[1] *Monetary Theory and the Trade Cycle*, p. 226 and p. 219.
[2] Cf. D. H. Robertson, *Money*, pp. 98, 99.

Once again, then, Dr. Hayek insists that it is the change in the relative values of future and present goods caused by an artificially created flow of credit which perpetuates disequilibrium. The price of present goods can remain unchanged throughout; but if future goods are cheapened relatively through technical changes, then, if artificial credit support is added, over-production of future goods is bound to be revealed when the support is withdrawn. Forced savings merely add fuel to the flame.

APPENDIX 4

BIBLIOGRAPHY

1. Preliminary Reading

H. D. Henderson, *Supply and Demand* (Nisbet).

Committee on Finance and Industry: Report (Macmillan Report). Cmd. 3897 of 1931.

2. Intermediate List

For those who cannot pursue the matter to the bitter end, yet desire some knowledge of the original texts, the following are suggested. They represent a fairly adequate sample of the theories considered, and none of them is unduly obscure.

F. Lavington, *The Trade Cycle* (King), 1922.

R. G. Hawtrey, *Trade Depression and the Way Out* (Longmans), new edition, 1933.

F. A. Hayek, *Monetary Theory and the Trade Cycle* (Cape), 1932.

G. Haberler, *Lecture on "Money and the Business Cycle"* in *Gold and Monetary Stabilisation* (University of Chicago Press), 1932.

D. H. Robertson, *Money* (Nisbet), 1928.

J. M. Keynes, *Treatise on Money*, vol. i. Bks. III. and IV. (Macmillan), 1930.

J. A. Hobson, *The Economics of Unemployment* (Allen and Unwin), 1931.

Royal Institute of International Affairs, *Monetary Policy and the Depression* (Oxford), 1933.

3. LIST BY CHAPTERS OF TEXT

Chapter I

Wesley C. Mitchell, *Business Cycles, The Problem and its Setting* (New York), 1927.

A. C. Pigou, *Industrial Fluctuations* (Macmillan), 2nd edition.

W. H. Beveridge, *Unemployment* (Longmans), 1930.

Sir Arthur Salter, *Recovery* (Bell), Cheap edition, 1933.

League of Nations, *World Economic Survey*, 1932–33.

Lionel Robbins, *The Great Depression* (Macmillan), 1934. (Contains a most comprehensive collection of statistics relating to the slump of 1929.)

Chapter II

Pigou, *op. cit.*

D. H. Robertson, *Study in Industrial Fluctuations* (King), 1915.

J. H. Kirk, *Agriculture and the Trade Cycle* (King), 1933.

W. S. Jevons, *Investigations in Currency and Finance* (Macmillan), 1884.

J. M. Clark, *Economics of Overhead Costs* (University of Chicago), 1923.

Chapter III

R. G. Hawtrey, *Currency and Credit*, 1928; *Trade and Credit*, 1928; *Art of Central Banking*, 1932; *Trade Depression and the Way Out*, 1933. (All Longmans.)

Chapter IV

F. A. Hayek—as quoted in List 2.

Chapter V

F. A. Hayek, *Prices and Production* (Routledge), 1931.

Haberler—as quoted in List 2.

Böhm-Bawerk, *Positive Theory of Capital* (trans. Smart) (Macmillan), 1891.

Chapters VI and VII

Robertson—as quoted in List 2; *Banking Policy and the Price Level* (King), 1932.

J. M. Keynes, *Treatise on Money* (2 vols.) (Macmillan), 1930.

Cassel, *Theory of Social Economy* (Fisher Unwin), 1923.

Chapter VIII

Hobson—as quoted in List 2; *Rationalisation and Unemployment* (Allen and Unwin), 1930.

E. F. M. Durbin, *Purchasing Power and Trade Depression* (Cape), 1933. (Especially for other under-consumption theories.)

Chapter IX

Lavington—as quoted in List 2.

Pigou—as quoted for Chapter I.

W. Macdougall, *Psychology* (Home University Library), 1914.[1]

M. Ginsberg, *The Psychology of Society* (Methuen), 1924.

W. H. R. Rivers, *Instinct and the Unconscious* (Cambridge), 1924.

B. Hart, *Psychopathology* (Cambridge), 1929.

A. Adler, *Understanding Human Nature*, trans. 1932.

Chapter X

Wesley C. Mitchell—as quoted for Chapter I.

Sir Arthur Salter and others, *The World's Economic Crisis*

---

[1] There is, of course, a literature of psychology. The books mentioned may, however, suffice as an introduction.

(Unwin Brothers), 1932 (various suggestions as to remedies).

J. M. Clark, *Strategic Factors in Business Cycles* (New York), 1934. (Develops an interesting distinction between causes which can and causes which cannot be controlled.)

Barbara Wootton, *Plan or No Plan* (Gollancz), 1934.

(An interesting and stimulating investigation of the issue raised, but not followed up, at the end of this volume.)

Printed in Great Britain by R. & R. CLARK, LIMITED, *Edinburgh.*